You Too Can
DRAW

Nicola Sedgwick

**MENTOR
BOOKS**

First Published 2003
by
MENTOR BOOKS
43 Furze Road,
Sandyford Industrial Estate,
Dublin 18.
Tel. +353 1 295 2112/3   Fax. +353 1 295 2114
e-mail: admin@mentorbooks.ie
www.mentorbooks.ie

ISBN: 1-84210-202-8

Illustrations by Nicola Sedgwick
Cover by Graham Thew

Printed in Ireland by ColourBooks
1 3 5 7 9 10 8 6 4 2

To my Mother and Father
who encouraged my creativity from an early age

Much appreciation and thanks to Danny McCarthy, head of Mentor Books, who gave invaluable advice, support, suggestions and encouragement throughout the book's lengthy development.

Thanks in abundance to Claire Haugh, whose editing was excellent and meticulous, and whose eagle eye missed nothing!

Many thanks to Kathryn McKinney for her creative and professional design work.

To the great staff at Mentor Books – thanks for everything!

To the National Gallery of Ireland, for permission to reproduce *Military Manoeuvres* by Richard Moynan.

Thanks to artist friends and associates who freely and graciously offered gems of wisdom and gave astute assessment: Peter Collis, Tom Roche, Don Conroy, John Coyle, Maurice de Cogan, Anne Kennedy, Wendy Shea.

Grateful thanks to Bernadette Murphy SSL, Lauren Dwyer and Maeve Hunter for advice and assessment.

Many thanks to the life-drawing models, especially Gerry and Anne Sedgwick, Irene Kellett, Una Whelan, Sadbh Gannon and Jason Mahony.

And to all my dear friends and family, who helped me to stay grounded and motivated!

CONTENTS

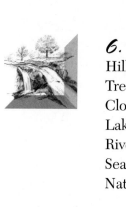

INTRODUCTION

You too can draw!

Yes, it is true. If you follow all the guidelines given in this book you will have at your disposal a lifelong skill – to be able to draw!

Creating realistic pictures involves drawing what you SEE rather than drawing what you THINK you see. Many of us do not realise that when we draw an object we do not look at it properly, and do not think out its dimensions and angles and interrelations with other objects.

Chapter 1 will give you guidelines on materials etc. The various methods presented in Chapter 2 will shift your perspective so you can see objects in a new light, and in doing so draw them more accurately by introducing ideas such as measuring, scribbling and using grids.

And of course it doesn't stop there! Chapter 3 introduces you to several techniques which will further enhance your drawing ability, such as the art of shading, composition and the use of perspective. Chapters 4–9 is where it gets really interesting, as this is where you put all your new knowledge into practice! You are carefully guided through various subjects which include the human figure, animals, nature and animation. You are also frequently given page references to techniques and methods whenever necessary. These latter chapters may also give you an idea of where you would most like to focus your attention and time in the future.

But . . . before you begin to draw . . .

- Please learn the methods in Chapter 2 before you practise exercises elsewhere!
- Remember that there may be times when you will get frustrated with a drawing or picture. This is perfectly normal – all artists experience this. It often occurs when you are actually discovering something new, so don't give up! Your patience will be rewarded with a great sense of achievement.
- As you experiment, let your own style develop, and give your imagination free rein. Both these qualities will emerge and grow the more you draw.
- Look out for **HOT TIPS** throughout the book. These are special creativity tips to really add sparks to your work.

Very best wishes for your future artistic
endeavours and adventures!

Nicola Sedgwick

Chapter 1
Getting Started

◼ Pencils

In this book for the most part you will be using good old ordinary **pencils**, which can be found in most stationery and art shops. Pencils are coded according to their hardness or softness.
- 8B is very dark and soft.
- 4H is quite light and very hard.
- HB, B and 2B are the pencils mostly used in this book as they are mid-tone, carry good definition and are suitable for shading.

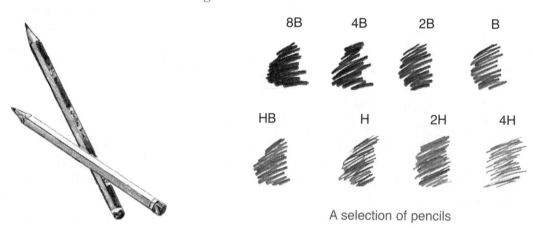

A selection of pencils

◼ Erasers & Sharpeners

You can get good **pencil erasers** from your local art or stationery shop. Don't be tempted to buy cheap versions as they do not erase well.

When you are correcting a small area of a drawing with an eraser, you may find you are rubbing out areas of the drawing surrounding it. In a case like this you can cut out a small piece from the eraser, and use it to correct the mistake.

Pencil sharpeners are a must! I recommend that you get a sharpener that stores pencil pearings, which saves you lots of bother. And again, be sure to get a good quality sharpener.

Basic Shading

When you finish a drawing you may want to shade it in. Shading can make an outline drawing extremely lifelike and three-dimensional. Let's have a look at three types: single hatching, cross hatching and blending.

SINGLE HATCHING

Draw the outline with a HB pencil and shade with a 2B. Draw the pencil strokes beside each other and all facing the same way. Remember to follow the natural angle of the object you are shading. To achieve darker shading, just shade over the previously shaded area again.

CROSS HATCHING

As its name suggests, this is a combination of two sets of single hatching, drawn at opposite angles to each other.

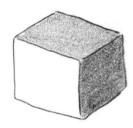

BLENDING

Blunt the sharp tip of the 2B pencil by rubbing it on spare paper. Then draw soft strokes one beside the other on your drawing so the strokes don't show.

For even smoother blending rub the shading with your finger. The blurry pencil marks may go outside the lines of your object so just use an eraser to get rid of these after you finish.

If you are shading a curved object using single hatching or cross hatching draw the pencil strokes following the contours of the object. This gives the object a realistic three-dimensional effect.

Hot Tip

Did you know that when shading in drawings, left-handed artists draw single hatching slanted to the left and right-handed artists draw to the right? Can you tell if I am right or left-handed? Look at other drawings in the book to help you guess.

Left-handed artists   Right-handed artists

■ *Markers and Technical Pens*

When you finish a drawing, you can give it a sharp and definite outline by using permanent markers or technical pens.

- **Permanent black markers** – come in point sizes ranging from very 0.1 (fine) to 1.00 (thick).
- **Technical pens** – give a nice clean crisp line. The most convenient type to buy are the ones that take **cartridges**. Point sizes you can start off with are 0.18, 0.25 (both quite fine) and 0.35 (medium).

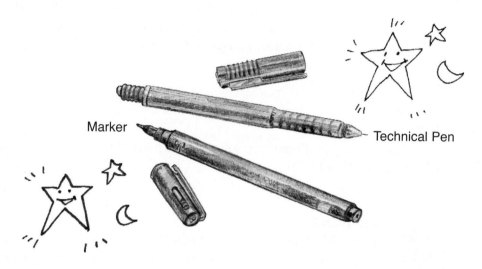

Marker

Technical Pen

■ *Paint and Palettes*

BLACK PAINT

Black paint can be used to good effect in your drawing either as a wash or as a solid block of opaque (non-see-through) colour.

- If black is to be used as a wash, buy a good **watercolour** black and use a tiny blob in a good deal of water before mixing and applying to the picture. This will produce a shade of grey which you can paint over again and again in further washes if you wish to get darker shades.

- If black is to be used as an opaque colour, **gouache** (designers' watercolour) is recommended. Just a little water is needed to mix the paint to a good consistency.

WHITE PAINT

- **White gouache** is excellent to cover pen or marker mistakes. If your drawing paper is white as opposed to a creamy shade, the correction will be nearly invisible. As with the black gouache, mix with a little water to get an opaque consistency.
- Marker lines can sometimes seep through white paint. If this happens apply one layer of paint over the marker line and allow it to dry before applying another layer.

Plastic palettes are suitable for working with both watercolour and gouache.

■ Brushes

There is a good range of medium-priced **watercolour brushes** available in all art shops. I suggest you get brushes that are sable/synthetic mix, and for now all you need are sizes 2, 4 and 6. Don't buy cheap brushes because it is often difficult to get a nice point on their tips. These types of brushes can also become hairy and useless within a short period of time.

Always remember to wash your brush after use and do not leave it sitting in water!

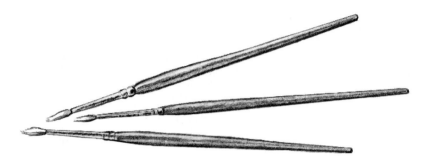

■ Paper

When doing rough sketches you do not need to work on fine quality **paper**. You can use lots of different kinds of layout paper, coloured paper as well as photocopy paper (which I do a lot!). Of course you can also use standard **A4 or A3 size sketchpads** that you can pick up in art shops.

Note: Newspaper paper is a little too thin to work on.

For more finished work get **cartridge paper**, either as sketchpads or large A1 size single sheets which you can cut to whatever size you want.

- If you are doing paint washes use thick paper, as thinner paper tends to buckle. You can also use a smooth watercolour paper or board.
- Say you have finished a drawing and want to fill in areas with watercolour washes or gouache. If you are afraid of making a mistake on the original you can photocopy the picture onto another sheet of cartridge or watercolour paper and then work on the copy. Make sure the copier gives you a crisp image and that the sheets of paper are thin enough to go through the machine.

Hot Tip

Here is how you draw a straight line . . .
When we draw, most of us automatically hold a pencil in the same way we hold a pen to write, as in A. Yes, me too! If you want to draw a straight line, however, hold the pencil as seen in B. Draw your line, bringing your arm back towards you very slowly as you do so. It's magic!

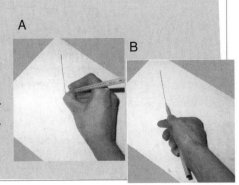

■ *How to develop roughs to finished artwork*

USING A LIGHTBOX

This is the method I use most often. I find it very handy and there is no need for erasers.

- Draw your first rough. When it gets messy or overworked, then it's time for a new rough.
- Switch on your lightbox and tape your first rough onto the surface. Use invisible tape or sticky post-it note paper as they are easy to remove later.
- Tape a fresh blank sheet on top of your first rough. Make sure you can see through the blank page to the drawing underneath.
- Develop the next rough by redrawing the first rough and making any further changes needed.
- You can now remove this final page from the lightbox and work up shading and detail.

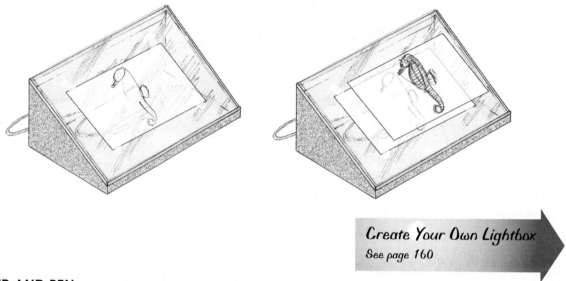

Create Your Own Lightbox
See page 160

PAPER AND PEN

You can use this method when you are quite confident in drawing a certain object, and only need to make minimal changes to your rough.

- Draw your rough very lightly. Then go over it again, making changes until you are satisfied with the shape.
- Then redraw an outline over your rough, using marker or technical pen.
- Rub out all your pencil lines.

First rough   Rough with technical pen added   Final drawing with pencil lines removed

Chapter 2

The Essential Methods

Overview

- The methods in this chapter will give you a special knowledge that will last a lifetime. As you know from learning any new skill, mastery of it takes time. Be patient with yourself, and most importantly, practise as much as possible, because you must know the basic structure of drawing before you can progress. Yehudi Menuhin, the violinist, didn't become a brilliant violinist by practising only once every few weeks!
- Bring a small sketchbook with you everywhere and draw any object, anywhere, anytime. It doesn't matter whether it is a salt cellar or a tree – just get drawing!
- You can use any of the following methods with any subject you draw in the future. It is up to you to decide which ones suit you best.

PREPARATORY EXERCISE

FREEHANDING

This first exercise introduces you to your pencil and paper.

From your selection of pencils, choose one and draw lots of lines, circles and a variety of different shapes. Alternate leaning heavily and lightly on your pencil to create lines of different strengths. Now try out different pencils, drawing shapes with them all. Don't be afraid to use the full page of your paper – when people first begin drawing they often limit themselves to a small portion of a page.

    If you find you are beginning to doodle or draw designs and objects, that's great! You are already awakening your creativity.

THE METHODS

CONTOUR DRAWING

This is a method often used to awaken the creative side of the brain.

- First draw your non-drawing hand as best you can (without tracing around it!). Later, when you draw your hand using contour drawing, you will be able to compare and contrast drawing your normal way and drawing this new way.

- Make sure that your paper/sketchpad is secure and will not move around on your table or desk.

- Now draw your non-drawing hand again, but this time look at it **THE WHOLE TIME** while your pencil draws on the paper. The trick here is to **SEE** your hand not as a hand but as a series of lines and curves.

- Take your time and concentrate as you draw. You should end up with something like the drawing on the right.

- If you want to do a more accurate drawing using a 'modified' contour drawing method, allow yourself to look at your sketchpad now and again. This could apply if you have to lift your pencil to a different place, for example, adding fingernails on a hand.

You will get better and better the more you practise. Start with simple objects first such as fruit, plants, household items and books. This method is a good start in showing you how to draw what you **SEE** instead of drawing what you **THINK** you see.

Always start a drawing in an area where you feel the easiest lines and angles can be seen.

MEASURING

The mechanics of measuring is used all the time by artists, as it is an excellent tool in achieving accuracy in drawings. Measuring is used when drawing from a photograph or picture, or when drawing from observation (drawing from a real object before you).
We will look at three types:

- Finger Measuring
- Touch Measuring
- Air Measuring

Note: Measuring is used in connection with other methods, as you will see over the next few pages.

■ *Finger Measuring*

WORKING FROM A PICTURE OR PHOTOGRAPH

Here we have a picture of an apple.
Using finger measuring you want to copy it as best you can.

Step 1

Measure the size of the apple by putting the finger and thumb of your non-drawing hand at the top and bottom of the apple as shown.

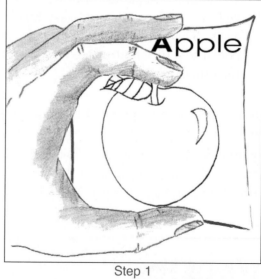

Step 1

14

Step 2

Then put your finger and thumb down on your drawing paper, still holding the measured position, and draw a circle as best you can joining both finger distances.

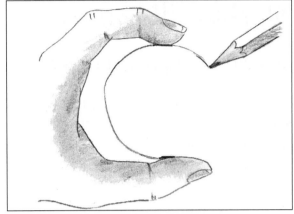

Step 2

Step 3

Lightly draw a temporary vertical line down the centre of your rough circle-apple. Dividing up an object with an **indicator line** like this gives you a better idea of where everything is positioned.

Using Indicator Lines
See page 19

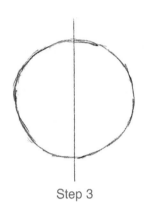

Step 3

Step 4

Now you want to add the stalk. Go back and look at the picture of the apple and finger measure from the top of the stalk to where the stalk joins the top of the apple.

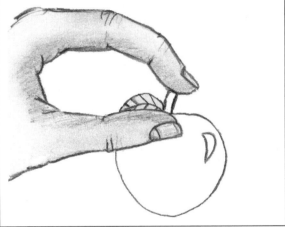

Step 4

Step 5

With the measured distance held within your fingers, go to your rough drawing and make **markers** (A and B) to show the top of the stalk. Markers are short indicator lines.

Step 6

Do the same procedure again to get the distance from the top of the apple to where the stalk finishes. Make another marker (C) to indicate the bottom of the stalk. Then draw the entire stalk.

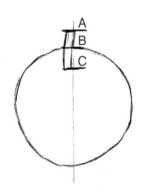

Steps 5 & 6

■ *Touch Measuring*

WORKING FROM A PICTURE OR PHOTOGRAPH

Great! You have roughed out most of your apple by finger measuring. Let's continue the drawing using touch measuring.

Step 7

Start by **refining** the shape of your apple. Go to the picture of the apple and run the finger of your non-drawing hand around its shape a few times.

Then put your non-drawing finger at a certain point along the apple's edge. Position your pencil at the same place on your own rough apple. Start moving your finger around the apple slowly and move your pencil on the paper at the same time. You can stop every now and then to check how you are doing.

Step 7

Step 8

Go back and make alterations and changes until you are satisfied. See the refined shape of the apple shown here.

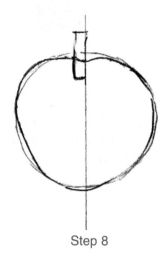

Step 8

Step 9

Then put your non-drawing hand at a certain point along the edge of the stalk. Position your pencil at the same place on your own rough drawing. As before, move your finger around the stalk slowly and move your pencil on the paper at the same time.

Tidy up the rough shape of the apple, using the lightbox, so you can see everything better as you progress.

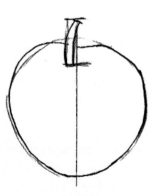

Step 9

16

Step 10

Next is the leaf. Once more go back and look at the original picture of the apple. You'll see that the leaf joins the stalk near the top of the apple. Put a little marker at this point on your own apple.

Now with your non-drawing hand, run your finger backwards and forwards over the top curve of the leaf of the original apple. When you are ready, touch measure this portion of the leaf.

Step 10

Step 11

Repeat the process by running your finger over the bottom curve of the leaf and touch measuring the line.

Check the correct width of the leaf by finger measuring first on the original picture and then on your own drawing.

Step 11

Step 12

Touch measure the middle line of the leaf.

Count the number of leaf veins and put markers for them evenly down the middle line. Then draw the veins on either side.

Step 12

Step 13

Lastly, add the highlight on the apple using finger measuring. Your apple is now complete. Well done!

Highlights
See page 37

Step 13

■ *Air Measuring 1*

WORKING FROM OBSERVATION – LIFE DRAWING

Air measuring differs from finger measuring only in that you cannot touch the object you are measuring.

Here we have a seated man as an example of an object/figure to be drawn from real life. The first thing you want to do is get the correct measurement for each section of the body. How you decide to do this will depend on how far away the figure is from you.

1. IF THE FIGURE IS FAR AWAY

Step 1

You may be able to air measure the whole body using your finger and thumb as shown. This way you get your markers for the top and bottom of your figure.

Step 1

Step 2

With your fingers still held in position (very important!) go to your sketchpad and draw your markers.

Step 3

These markers clearly show you what space you are working within.

If you want, you can draw a loose oval, as seen here, to indicate the overall shape.

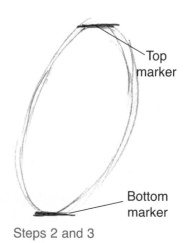

Top marker

Bottom marker

Steps 2 and 3

Step 4

Air measuring with your fingers, draw a **rounded shape** for the head. Now measure the distance from the chin to the shoulders and roughly draw in the neck.

In the same way, air measure and draw another rounded shape for the torso.

Rounded Shapes
See page 24

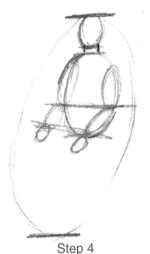

Step 4

Step 5

Continue air measuring the figure and adding rounded shapes for the rest of the body.

Using Indicator Lines: As a working example, look at your seated live model and move your pencil along the angle between the two elbows. Take note of the angle – then draw the indicator line at the same angle over the two elbows on your developing drawing.

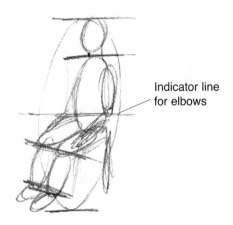

Indicator line for elbows

Step 5

Step 6

Introduce more detail over the rounded shapes.

Note: The eventual outline and finished drawing are shown overleaf.

Step 6

2. IF THE FIGURE IS NEARER

Step 1

Air measure section by section using your thumb and finger. For example, measure the head first, then from shoulder to waist, from waist to knees and finally from knees to feet. Then do the chair!

Step 1

Step 2

Draw the indicator lines first and then the head shape, using **scribbling**. Repeat this process, progressing through the body until it is all roughed out.

Scribbling
See page 25

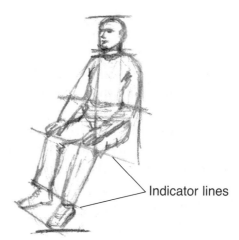

Indicator lines

Step 2

Steps 3 & 4

The finished figure. Step 3 shows the tidied-up outline drawing, and Step 4 shows the addition of detail and shading.

Step 3

Step 4

Hot Tip

Don't worry about details until you come to the final stages. It is important to get the overall shapes right first!

■ *Air Measuring 2*

WORKING FROM OBSERVATION – STILL LIFE

A. Draw it the size you want.
B. Draw it exactly the size you see it.

A. STILL LIFE – THE SIZE YOU WANT

- You may want the still life to fit the size of your sketchpad or a more specific size. See the three sketchpads below as examples.

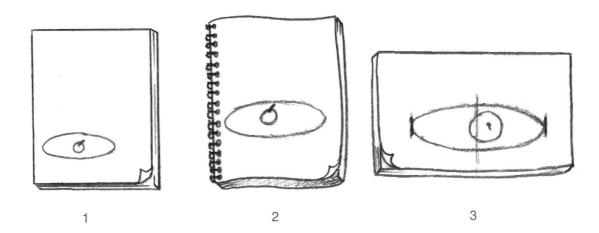

1   2   3

- For this exercise, I want to draw the still life on Sketchpad 3, since this particular still life seems to lend itself naturally towards a landscape shape. I also want it to nearly fill the page.

- Because of this it's a good idea to draw the plate first, as it shows the entire width of the still life. We'll go through the procedure step by step on the next page.

Hot Tip

See the different sizes of the sketchpads above? The shape of the first two sketchpads is called 'portrait' (it is shaped longer than wide) and the third is called 'landscape' (it is shaped wider than long). These shapes are so called because portraits are usually painted on the first two types and landscapes on the third type.

Step 1

Make markers for either side of the plate, and then draw a rough oval.

Next, lightly draw a vertical and horizontal indicator line halfway through the plate. These lines will help define where the fruit will be placed.

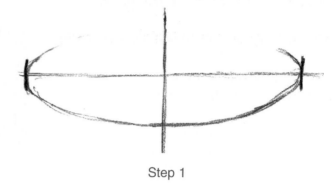

Step 1

Step 2

Notice as you look at the original still life that the apple is almost all on the right side of the vertical line and about halfway up the horizontal.

Air measure and draw the apple, checking its position is accurate.

It is important to get the first object right as all other items will be drawn in relation to it.

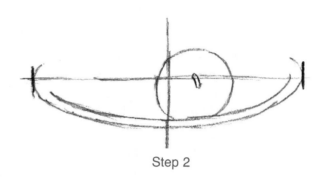

Step 2

Step 3

With a pencil held in front of your still life, air measure the angles between pieces of fruit in the original still life. Move the pencil back and forth to check the angle. On your sketchpad draw in the indicator lines and put markers where the tops or bottoms of fruit are. Then draw in the fruit.

Remember: When you are drawing indicator lines like this you may have to correct them a few times. Don't worry if this happens – you can't expect to get everything right first time round!

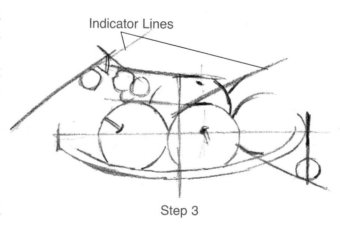

Indicator Lines

Step 3

Step 4

Continue building up the drawing until it is completed.

The eventual outline and finished drawing are shown overleaf.

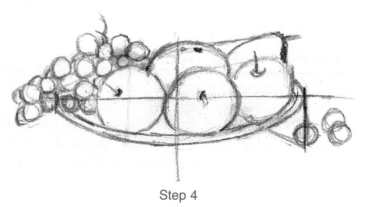

Step 4

B. STILL LIFE – THE SIZE YOU SEE IT

Step 1

Get your finger and thumb into action and air measure what you think is the easiest fruit to draw first. In this case we'll choose the same apple as before.

Draw it roughly on your sketchpad.

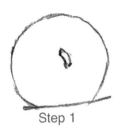

Step 1

Step 2

The trick here is to work outwards, by measuring the fruit directly surrounding the apple, and then the fruit surrounding that fruit.

The reason for this is that you will have a really good idea of where each piece of fruit is positioned. Instead of say, drawing the grapes first, then one of the apples – chances are if you do not measure correctly the fruit will not all fit together properly!

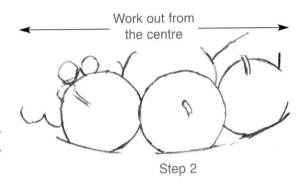

Work out from
the centre

Step 2

Step 3

Add indicator lines to check the correct alignments as you progress.

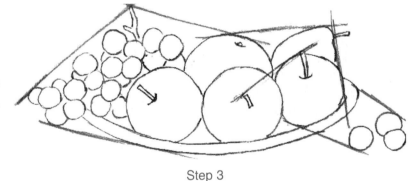

Step 3

Step 4

When everything is in the right place, tidy up. Add shading and finer details by checking back to the original still life picture for reference.

Step 4

ROUNDED SHAPES

Roughing out drawings by using rounded shapes is a great technique to use, especially when drawing from your imagination or memory. Of course you can also use it when working from observation! It offers you a basis on which you can build up, refine and alter the objects you wish to draw before doing the final artwork.

The rounded shapes method is ideal to use with organic objects such as fruit, the human figure and animals.

FISHY BUSINESS

Step 1

Begin by drawing a simple oval. An oval is chosen because it is the basic shape of the object required.

Step 2

Develop the rough of a fish. On your rough add fins and define where the face is.

Step 3

To finish the drawing, tidy up and add some more details and a little shading.

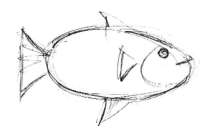
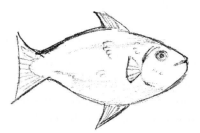

FLYING THE FLAG

Step 1

Using rounded shapes create the rough of a human figure. The only areas which are not rounded shapes are a few necessary connecting lines for body parts, as seen in the neck and hip areas.

Step 2

Add detail to her hair, face and clothes. Add the flag to your rough.

Step 3

To finish the drawing, tidy up and add some more details and a little shading.

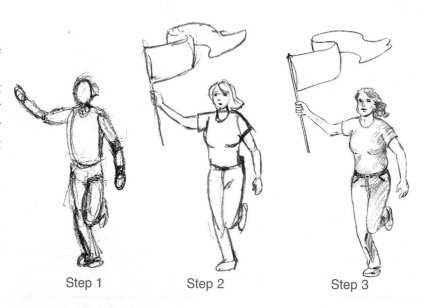

Step 1   Step 2   Step 3

Hot Tip

Before you attempt drawing from imagination or memory, make sure you know your subject very well.

24

SCRIBBLING

When scribbling from real life, from imagination or from memory, a drawing is begun by sketching out rough lines and shapes, and developing the general feel and shape of the object. This is done until the right shape is achieved. Only then is the rough tidied up.

KEY OF THE DOOR
The rough of this key was scribbled from observation. As you can see there were some areas that needed correction before the final drawing.

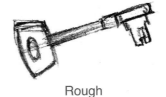

Rough   Finished drawing

WAITER WALKING
The waiter was drawn from imagination. Notice the different placings of his left arm in the rough before deciding on its final position. You may also notice the cap is left out in the finished drawing and a money pouch added to his waist instead!

Rough   Finished drawing

TAPE DISPENSER
The tape dispenser, drawn from observation, was done using a mixture of rounded shapes and scribbling. A little air measuring was also used.

Rough   Finished drawing

NEGATIVE SPACE

When using negative space as a technique, instead of drawing the lines of an object and all the details that are inside, you look at the space or spaces that surround the object and draw them. You are drawing a picture from the outside in!

SIMPLE SHAPES

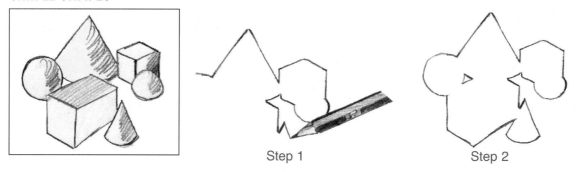

Step 1   Step 2

Here you can see a selection of simple shapes being drawn using negative space. The objects can then be completed to resemble the initial picture.

TEENAGE THRILLER

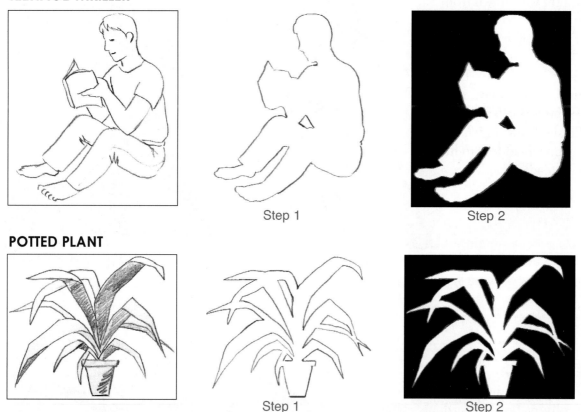

Step 1   Step 2

POTTED PLANT

Step 1   Step 2

The seated young man and the pot plant show different steps of drawing with negative space: **Step 1** is the finished pencil outline, **Step 2** is how the negative space looks when the drawing is reversed in black.

Drawing negative shapes is just another example of seeing in a different way. Remember, you are always drawing LINES and CURVES and not NAMED OBJECTS like people or plants.

VISUAL MEMORY

We are well used to using our brain to memorise areas of text.
It follows that we can train our visual memory in exactly the same way!
The two exercises below will get you started.

TABLE TOP

Step 1

Put a few objects before you on a table. Make sure they are simple in shape.

Concentrate intently on them for a few minutes. Note where they touch or overlap, their size differences and general shapes.

Step 1

Step 2

Take your paper and pencil and draw the objects from memory. Don't look up to check the objects as you draw!

When you are finished, compare your drawing with the objects in front of you. If you have made no mistakes, well done! However, it is also very interesting to see where you may have gone wrong. The most common reason is that you had a lapse in concentration.

Step 2

Step 3

Redraw the incorrect parts this time by looking back and forth at the objects on the table and checking everything is OK as you finish it off.

PEOPLE WAITING

Step 1

Go to a bus stop, train station, shopping mall or busy street. Position yourself where you can safely observe people without them noticing you looking at them!

Step 2

Pick someone who is still for a few moments. Visually memorise as many features as you can (for example, clothes, bags, posture). Then go somewhere where you can sit down with your sketchpad, and draw the person as best you can. You'll be surprised at how well you do!

Step 3

If you can't get some features right, enlist the help of a friend or relative to pose in the same position as your chosen subject.

CIRCULAR AND SQUARE SHAPES

■ *Cylinders and Ellipses*

MUG OF COFFEE

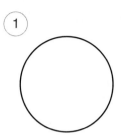

- If you look down on a round object, like a mug, a cup or a glass, you would see something like Picture 1 – a perfect circle!

- Most of the time in real life, however, you will see round objects at an angle. See how Picture 2 is a cylinder.

  A cylinder is defined as a solid or hollow body with circular equal ends and parallel sides.

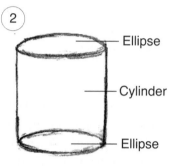

- Look at the circles at the top and bottom of the cylinder. These shapes are ellipses.

  An ellipse is defined as an oval shape resembling a flattened circle.

- Notice how the vertical lines are slightly curved where they meet the ellipses.

- To transform the cylinder into a mug (Picture 3), erase the top of of the lower ellipse. Then add a handle.
- Draw a smaller ellipse for the liquid in the mug. Add shading with slightly rounded lines to give the mug substance and depth.

NOW YOUR TURN

- Practise drawing cylinders and ellipses!

PACKET OF BISCUITS

- Here is an elongated cylinder. It helps if you draw an indicator line evenly along the middle, as this means you can check each ellipse is aligned with the next.

You can see how the cylinder is developed into a packet of biscuits. Note how the writing follows the cylinder's natural contours.

DRINKING BOTTLE

- Here is the rough and final drawing of a drinks bottle. See that the lid and lower part of the object are cylinders.
  Note: Adding shading and detail to a finished outline drawing gives it a realistic appearance.

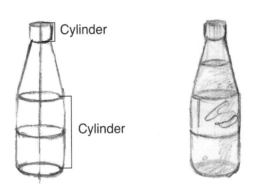

- What shape is the other part of the bottle, if it is not a cylinder?

  Well, if you draw two lines on the bottle that follow the ellipses as they decrease in size . . . you get a cone! The top part of the bottle is a cone with the top cut off.

A cone is a geometric shape consisting of a circular or oval base, tapering to a point.

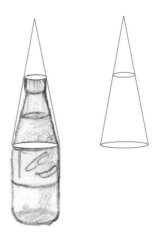

EYE SPY

- Here is a rough and finished drawing of a telescope in use. See how the basic shape is a cone cut off at the pointed end.

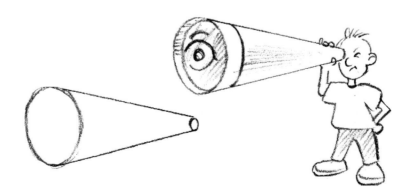

■ *Rectangles and Parallelograms*

- If we look at box shapes head on or from above they look like this: a square or rectangle.

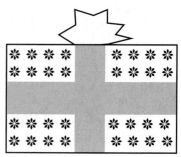

Rectangle dressed up as a gift box!

- However, as with circular shapes, we usually look at squares and rectangles from an angle, and then they look like the three-dimensional shapes shown here.

- Each side or face of these shapes is a parallelogram.

  A parallelogram has opposite sides that are parallel and of equal length.

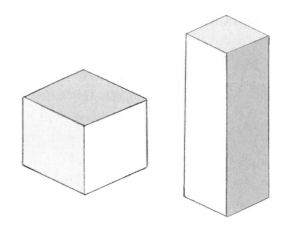

BLOCKBUSTER

Step 1

- Let's draw a book, starting from a rough parallelogram.

Step 1

Step 2

- Draw another parallelogram shape, with the same dimensions, a little distance below the first.

  Now draw in vertical connecting lines to make a box shape.

  Note: The lower box shape has been shaded here so you can see it more clearly.

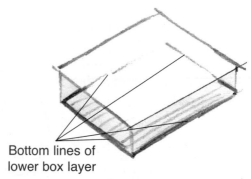

Bottom lines of lower box layer

Step 2

Step 3

- Then develop the book shape using the scribbling method. Notice how the title area on the cover has sides that are parallel to the sides of the book.

Step 3

Step 4

- Finally, tidy up and finish, adding details.

Step 4

Remember, each OPPOSITE side of a parallelogram is parallel!
See below lots of examples of parallelograms, some with connecting lines added and joined to identical parallelograms, creating various objects.
- Each of the sides of the shoebox that are parallel were drawn using different strengths and shading so you can identify them.

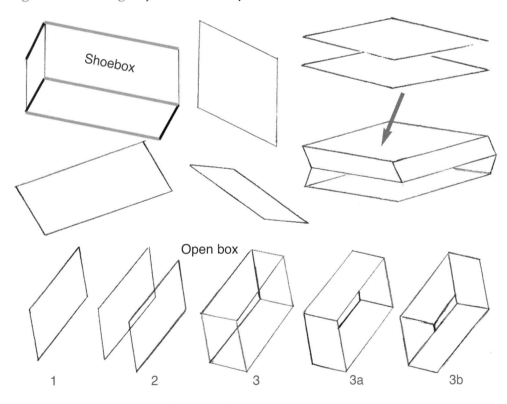

- An Open Box has been drawn in step-by-step stages. Look at Box 3 and see how it is developed into 3a and 3b, two different boxes.

GRIDS

Grids can be a helpful aid in getting correct dimension in a picture. You can use grids when drawing from observation or from photographs and pictures.

LANDSCAPE MADE EASY

Step 1

Get a piece of hard card, about 25mm x 20mm and cut a rectangle out of the centre as shown.

Step 2

Mark a series of horizontal and vertical marks around the edges. Then cut strips of string and stretch them across these lines to make a grid. Stick the string down with tape.

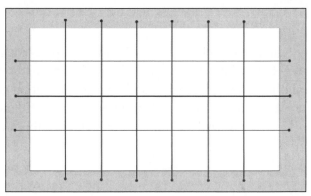

Step 3

Choose a scene that you want to draw. Let's say you are drawing a countryside scene similar to this one.

Step 4

Put the grid over the scene as shown. Now you can isolate each section of the picture and draw it in easy-to-manage stages!

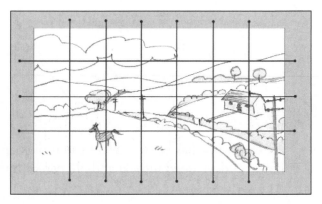

CORRECTING MISTAKES

You have made a mistake in your drawing but cannot pinpoint how exactly you went wrong and how you can correct it. The three methods below enable you to see your mistakes clearly and correct them with confidence.

Method 1

Hold your drawing up to a mirror. Because the mirror reverses everything, you literally see your picture in a different way – try it and see. You will be amazed that the mistakes are now clearly visible. Your eye will automatically go to the area that is not right.

Method 2

If you go away from your drawing for a while and then come back, you will see the picture with fresh eyes. But be warned! If you do not immediately note the areas that need correction, you will forget within minutes.

Method 3

If you have a lightbox, just turn your drawing over and look at it on the lightbox. Because of the light shining through your paper you will see your drawing from the reverse side. Again you will see your mistakes immediately.

No lightbox? Simply hold the paper up to a light, turning the page over as before. Remember, this can only work if your paper is thin enough to see through!

ENDNOTE

When you watch an artist drawing something perfectly on paper without any rough set-up you may think that you will never reach this lofty stage. But remember that the artist you are watching has spent years perfecting his or her art, and has probably drawn the object many times before!

Consider putting dates on all your drawings, so that you can look back and see how much you have progressed – and how you are developing into an artist!

Chapter 3
Terrific Techniques

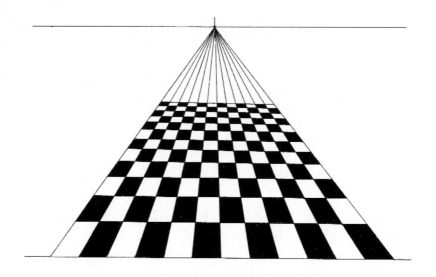

Overview

The following techniques are invaluable aids to constructing believable drawings after learning the basic methods of how to draw in the previous chapter. The knowledge of subjects such as composition, perspective and texture will greatly enrich the quality of your pictures and will enable you to view the world around you with a deeper artistic awareness.

LIGHT AND SHADE

Light creates shadows, which add an extra dimension to drawings.

It is helpful to know the names of the lit and shadowed areas situated on various parts of an object. The apple shown here is chosen as an example.

Light source is from the left

Look for the following:

A – The brightest light, the *highlight*.

B – The *ordinary light* falling on the surface of the apple.

C – The *surface shadow*, caused by light not being able to fall on this area.

D – A slight light at the edge of the apple, called a *reflection*, which is reflected brightness at the other edge of the surface shadow.

E – The *cast shadow* (E), darker than the surface shadow, which is created by the shadow projected by the apple onto the background.

F – This is the *dark crack* under the apple. It is the darkest shadow.

Highlights
See page 37

■ *Create your own Shadows*

JUICY APPLE

Step 1

Using a B pencil, draw the outline of the apple. Create a stronger line on the right side of the apple.

Rub your pencil tip on spare paper to blunt it, and then lightly shade over the apple except for the reflection area on the right. Then rub with your finger to get an even blend.

Step 1

Step 2

Using a 2B pencil, apply another level of shading on the right side of the apple, and blend again.

Shade in and blend the cast shadow on the ground.

Add a little shading to the leaf and stalk.

Step 2

Step 3

With the same 2B pencil, add extra shading to the leaf, and darken the area below the stalk.

Shade in the stalk and darken its right side.

Next, shade in the dark crack at the base of the apple, and add the highlight.

Step 3

■ *A Variety of Shadows*

SPRINTER

Note that the shadow below the sprinter's body is not connected to his feet – it is a little distance below. The position of the shadow shows how far off the ground he is.

STROLLER

In contrast to the sprinter above, the strolling girl's shadow is connected to her feet because at this point in her stride both feet are on the ground.

BEACHCOMBER

Here we see a person standing on a beach under the noon sun, and then later on in the afternoon sun.

Note how the shadow cast at noon is very short and under her feet because the sun is directly overhead.

In contrast the afternoon sun is much lower in the sky. This means the shadow cast is a good deal longer. The figure is standing at an angle to the sun so her shadow is at an angle too.

Interesting shadows can be seen at night-time when you stand in between streetlights, or as you walk from one streetlight to another.

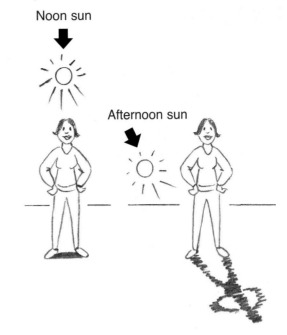

Create your own Highlights

Highlights bring an object to life.

A BUNCH OF GRAPES

Step 1

Draw a simple outline of a bunch of grapes. Add in the highlight shapes.

Step 2

Evenly shade the bunch of grapes, leaving white space for the reflected light. (Remember: This is the side **away** from the light source.)

Step 3

Shade in the darker surface shadows on the right of each grape, on top of the ordinary shadows. Finally, take a small piece off an eraser and slowly erase a selected area on each grape to create your highlight areas.

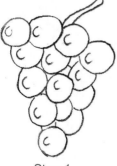

| Step 1 | Step 2 | Step 3 |

TEXTURE

Texture enhances the substance and form of drawings.

Copy this simple outline of a horse
and test the different textures below.

(1) Shading here is drawn in CURVED LINES and
blended shading.

(2) The outline is lightly drawn and over this
shading is applied in DOTS of varying intensity.

(3) Simple shading is done as a soft blend,
showing a few single HATCHED LINES.

(4) Here WOOD GRAINS are created in the horse
to make it look like a carving.

(5) The outline is not visible at all. The horse is a
series of strong HATCHED LINES.

(6) Broad areas of solid shading give the horse a
SHINY appearance.

WRINKLES AND FOLDS

To make textiles of any kind look realistic, it pays to add (when appropriate) wrinkles and folds.

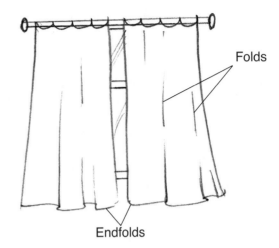

See how the **folds** and **end folds** have been drawn on these curtains. Notice that complete lines do not have to be drawn from top to bottom.

■ *End folds – from above*

It can often appear difficult to draw folds at the end of materials (e.g. curtains, coats, jumpers, skirts). In fact it is simpler than you think.

Step 1

Draw curvy lines like those shown here.

Step 2

Add lines downwards to connect with the outer edges of the front curves.

Step 3

Rub out the outer edges of the curves behind and your end folds are complete! If you like, you can shade the inner areas of the folds to create depth.

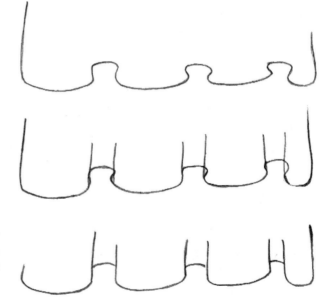

■ *End folds – from below*

Step 1

Draw larger curvy lines like those shown here. Compare these curves with the curves drawn 'from above'.

Step 2

Add lines downwards to connect with the outsides and insides of the curves. The inner areas are then shaded to give the impression of depth.

Wrinkles and folds in clothes

These fall into two basic categories:

1. HARD, CLEAR EDGES

These are mostly thin fabrics such as shirts and blouses, some dresses, light suits and trousers.

2. SOFT, ROUNDED EDGES

These are heavier materials such as jumpers, some anoraks and tracksuits.

Can you see the difference between the folds and wrinkles in the thin material of the shirt and the thick material of the jumper?

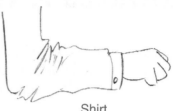

Shirt

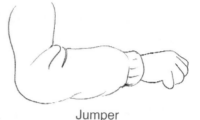

Jumper

TOPS AND BOTTOMS

Shading can be added to help define different types of clothing.

- The jumper the child is wearing produces soft folds, so the lines are softly curved. The shading is also soft and blended.
- The trousers the man is wearing are made of thinner material, producing crisper folds. The shading is also more clearly defined.

GREEK PHILOSOPHER

A great place to look for practising drawing folds is an illustrated book on ancient Greece and Rome!

The basic outline drawing is done first.

Then all the extra folds on the philosopher's robe are drawn in, as well as adding a lot of shading. The addition of extra folds and shading creates a greater impression of substance and depth.

Now try it yourself!

Outline   Finished drawing

COMPOSITION

*Composition is the art of combining the elements
of a picture so that it forms a satisfactory whole.*

Composition involves using a variety of elements in your picture, to create the overall effect of a pattern which pleases the eye. These elements include: balance, distance, cropping, grouping, perspective etc. It will all become clear as we go through each of the techniques on the following few pages!

Balance

See the simple picture below. There are several invisible diagonals here that help to produce a feeling of balance:
- The tree lower left and the sun upper right are balanced by the opposite diagonal of the shrub lower right and the clouds upper left.
- The path from lower left to mid right is also balanced by the sun as well as by the hill at left.
- The two smaller trees on the left are balanced by the two groups of trees on the right. If only two trees were on the right everything would look TOO ordered!
- The hill on the left is balanced by the three background hills that extend far right.

GENERAL NOTES
- Foreground items (in this case the tree and shrubs) are larger, darker and more detailed than those far away.
- We appear to be right in front of the foreground shrub. This is because we are too near to see the entire object. Remember, you don't have to draw a complete object in a picture for it to be recognisable!
- If you can, give two-thirds space to EITHER sky OR landscape when drawing a scene.
- If you put all the elements of your picture centred in the middle or just on one side of your picture it looks unbalanced – unless you are doing abstract/experimental art and are not bound by realism!
- Look up some paintings or drawings by artists that you like. Why do you like them? Can you see how artists balance their pictures?

Foreground and Background

*The area where people and objects are nearest to you in a picture
is called the foreground, and the area where people and
objects are far away is called the background.*

Look at *Military Manoeuvres* by Richard Moynan below. See how large the adults and children are in the foreground compared with those further away. Also note the buildings close by and in the distance.

The example of Oriental art below does not have a specific foreground or background, and the characters are roughly the same size. Pictures like these carry messages of symbolism and religious significance which peoples of their culture understand.

Distance and Illusion

FLOWER POWER

Look at the picture below. Yes, you can see that the same person is shown in different positions in a simple landscape: in the foreground, in the middle ground and in the background. Do you notice anything strange?

The 'giant' peeking its head over the mountain is the SAME SIZE as the person in the foreground. This surprise effect occurs because the two figures are placed in a setting that uses **perspective**.

Perspective
See page 48

Hot Tip

When lines touch as shown in Pictures 1 and 2, they don't look right to the viewer.

1 Head directly on line with mountain ✗

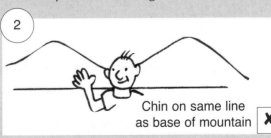

2 Chin on same line as base of mountain ✗

Instead:
- Change the position of the main subject so that these problems don't arise.
- And add a little space all around the main subject – this gives it room to breathe!

3 ✔

◼ *Artistic Licence*

Using artistic licence wisely can improve and enhance a picture.

SPOT THE DIFFERENCE
Can you see some of the changes made between the photograph and the drawing?
• The sky area has been expanded.
• A few clouds have been introduced.
• The cluster of the people on the pier has changed.
Can you see any other changes?

Note: Since the rope lines from the boat to the pier would not be visible in the drawing, they have been painted in white using a 0 (zero) brush to make them stand out.

Technical pen

Cutting Off / Cropping

WASHING DAY

Picture 1 – Here we see a young man putting his washing on a line. The picture is accurate, but for the purpose of this exercise we want the viewer of the picture to focus on the action.

Picture 2 – Here we see that we can do this by cutting off any unnecessary parts of the picture. See that even the top of his head need not be shown! The cropped image engages the viewer.

Picture 1

Picture 2

Using Space

You do not always have to fill every area of a picture to achieve a satisfactory end.

Less is actually more in this image of a snake in the desert. The message to the viewer is very strong but simple. And notice how the picture is balanced left to right.

▪ *Which Direction?*

A picture conveys a message to the viewer in a visual way. In the Western world people generally look at a picture from left to right. However, you can lead viewer's eyes the way you want.

COUNTRY DRIVE

The picture shown here achieves this by leading the viewer's eye up the road from bottom right upwards in the direction of the town on the horizon.

▪ *Dominance*

To make one object the main focus of your picture, create greater detail and strong lines around it. Putting the object in the foreground helps too!

EPIC JOURNEY

In the picture below our attention is drawn to the standing figure. Our eye goes first to the man, then to see what he is seeing: the faraway city, then back down the meandering river, and then up the cliff to the figure again . . .

Grouping

BIRTHDAY BOUQUET

Step 1

Draw a rough sketch of where the flowers in the bouquet will be, making sure they are all at different and interesting angles.

Step 2

Refine the rough, and draw flowers of the same type at a distance from each other. By doing this the picture is much more eyecatching.

Then add some background leaf shapes.

Step 3

You may want to move some of the items around to bring about a greater harmony.

Note: See if you can spot what has been changed from Step 2 to Step 3!

Add more leaves and then introduce shading to complete the picture.

PERSPECTIVE

Perspective drawing means getting a three-dimensional look on a two-dimensional surface. By using the following basics of perspective, you will be able to create pictures that have accurate and believable dimensions.

■ The Horizon Line

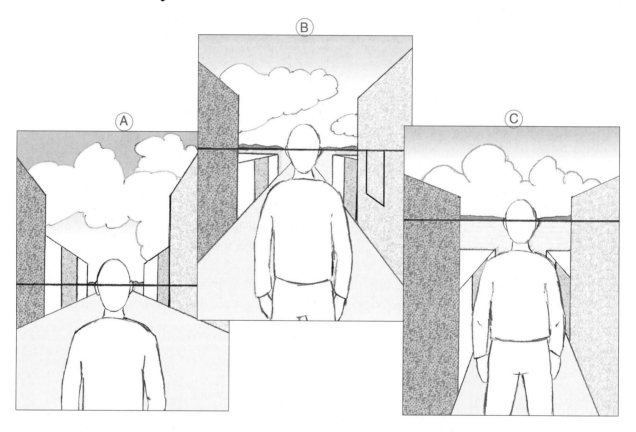

Here we see a person standing at different heights in a street with buildings that recede into the distance. Further away we see countryside and clouds in the sky.

First note the **horizon line** or **eye level**, which is the dark horizontal line drawn across the person's eyes. The horizon line is exactly that: how you view (at your eye level) any scene in relation to the far-off horizon. The buildings below the eye level slant downwards towards us and those above eye level slant upwards.

Picture A: The person is standing at a low height. Note how broad the angle of the street is and how much sky is visible in comparison with Picture C.

Picture B: The person is standing at a medium height. You can now see the tops of the low buildings on the left and right, and the far-off horizon has lifted.

Picture C: The person is standing at a great height. You can see much more of the countryside as the horizon is raised again. The angles at the tops of the buildings are not as slanted as before.

NOW YOUR TURN

Check the horizon line out for yourself! Go to a street or road. Look down it, observing lines and angles. Then crouch down and see how all these angles change.

■ *One-Point Perspective*

One-point perspective is viewing a scene in such a way that all the angled lines converge into one point in the distance.

Let's see how one-point perspective looks on a diagram, and learn the names of various lines.

- The *vanishing point* is the point on the horizon line where all lines meet.
- The lines that come from different angles and meet at the vanishing point are called *convergence lines*.
- If you are looking at an object directly at eye level, you will only see its front, as in BOX 1.
- If you are looking upward from the horizon line you will see the front, bottom and side of an object, as seen in BOX 2.
- When you are looking downward from eye level, you can see the front, top and side of an object, as seen in BOX 3.
- The convergence lines are the only lines that are **angled** in one-point perspective. All the other lines remain either horizontal or vertical.

In this diagram the convergence lines represent the sides of the boxes, while the horizontal and vertical lines represent the front and back areas of the boxes.

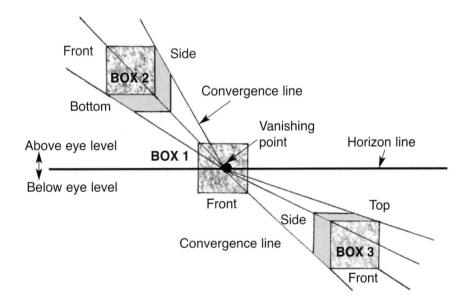

![Hot Tip]

YOUR HORIZON – MY HORIZON
If you are out in the open and look at the line where the sky meets the land or the sea, this is not only the horizon line for you, but also the horizon line for everyone no matter what their height. Even a pilot looking out from his aeroplane will have the same horizon line as you.

THE TILED FLOOR

Puzzle no more how chessboards or tiled floors are done in perspective!

Remember – Draw out everything first in light pencil. When you have finished your picture, you can then rub out the lines that you don't need.

Step 1

Draw the **horizon line** and then halfway along it draw a **vertical line** downwards. Now add a **horizontal line** some distance below.

Draw a series of **evenly** spaced round markers along the lower horizontal line. It is up to you how many markers to draw and how far apart.

Finally, draw a convergence line from each marker up to the vanishing point on the horizon line.

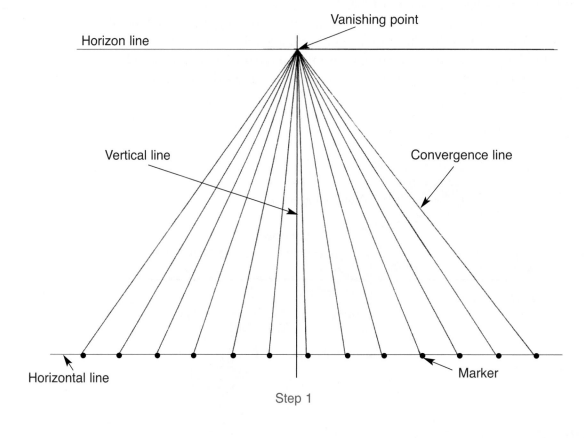

Step 1

Step 2

Draw an angled line from the last marker on the right end of the lower horizontal line. Continue this line all the way up to the left side of the horizon line. See how this line crosses over all the convergence lines.

Now place round markers at each crossover point, and draw horizontal lines through each of these markers and across all the convergence lines.

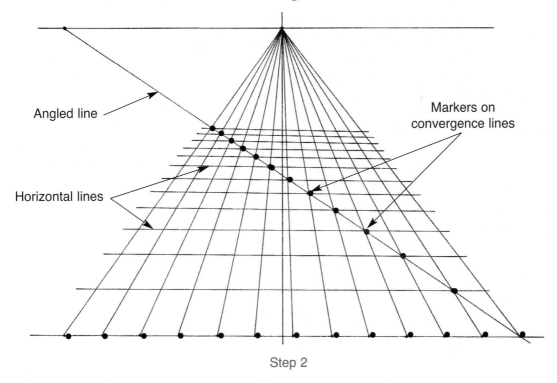

Step 2

Step 3

Fill in alternate squares with black pen or paint to create the chessboard effect and your picture is finished – almost! Don't forget to erase your temporary lines!

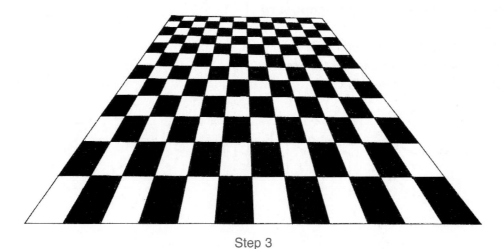

Step 3

THE ROOM

Now let's put one-point perspective into reality . . .

Stage 1

- Draw a horizontal line A (which is your horizon line) and a vertical line B. The vanishing point is C where the lines cross.
- Next, draw a square shape D. Its centre is C where A and B cross. This forms the walls, ceiling and floor of the room.
- Now add two more squares: E for the back wall, and F for the window.
- Draw convergence lines from the four corners of the largest square to meet at the vanishing point.

Stage 2

- Complete the window on the back wall.
- Insert G, H, I and J, parts or sides of objects from which you will draw convergence lines.

Stage 3

- Convergence lines can now be drawn from the shapes G – J to get the correct perspective.
- Only after these lines are done do you draw the far sides of the objects.

Stage 4

- The finished room, with all the temporary lines removed and extra detail added – including Fido!

How do you get a correct centre vertical line where the two doors of the cupboard meet?
- Draw two diagonal lines as seen in B below. The place where the lines cross is the centre.
- The final cupboard is shown in C.

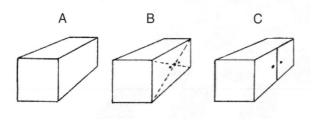

A   B   C

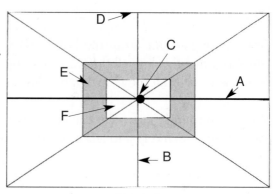

Stage 1

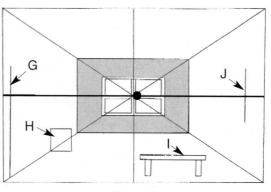

Stage 2

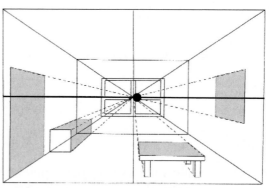

Stage 3

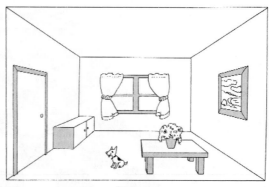

Stage 4

Two-Point Perspective

This technique is the same as one-point perspective, except now you have two vanishing points.

- Another diagram! Don't panic.
  If you look at the object below you will see that there are vertical lines but, apart from the horizon line there are **no horizontal lines** on top or bottom of objects. You are also looking at the FRONT CORNER of the object.

- Check out where your horizon line (eye level) is. From the front corner (vertical line A), draw lines D and E on either side until they hit the horizon line. Here then are your two vanishing points. Now you have to get the correct angles for the bottom of the object (see angled lines B and C).

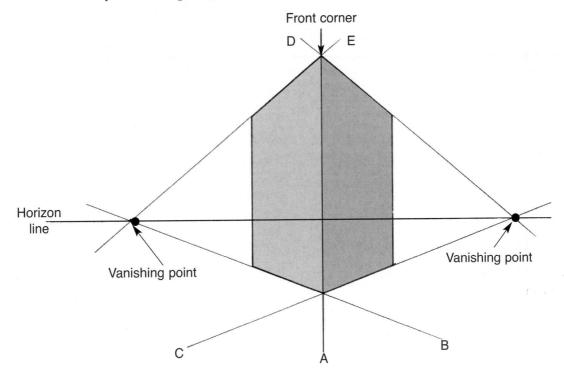

AN OFFICE BLOCK

Now let's put two-point perspective into reality . . .

Step 1

We start by drawing the front corner of the office building (vertical line). By drawing convergence lines to the two vanishing points on either side you can get correct angles for the buildings and their details.

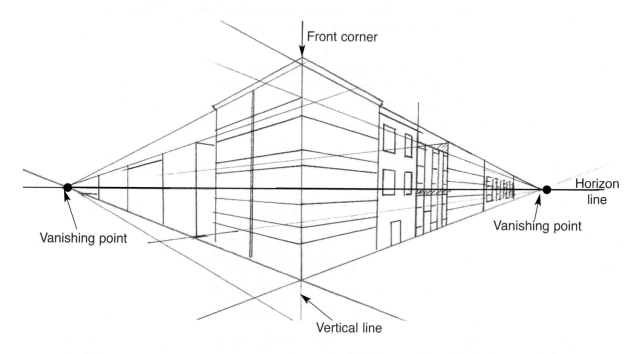

Step 2

It won't take you much time to build up a finished drawing like the one below. Add lots more detail than I have!

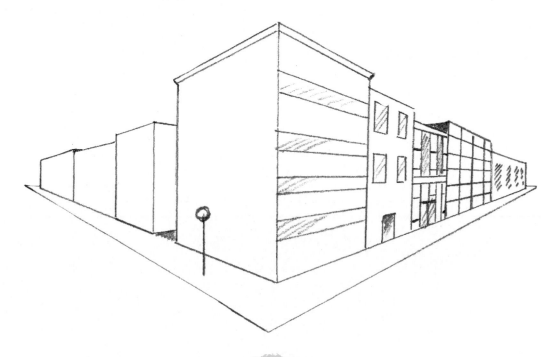

A COOL CAR

Step 1

Start by drawing the horizon line. Remember, the horizon line is always at your eye level. Decide where the front corner of your object is to be. Then draw lines A and B on either side until they hit the horizon line. These become your two vanishing points. Remember to use measuring, e.g. to get the distance between the front and back wheels and the angle of the front tyre.

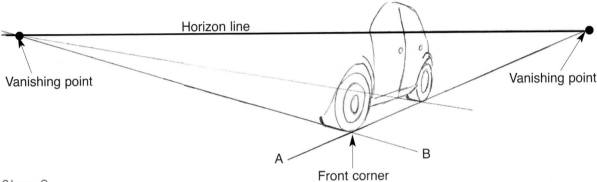

Step 2

Build up the car by drawing both freehand (using measuring!) and using the convergence lines with two-point perspective. This way you are assured of getting the angles right.

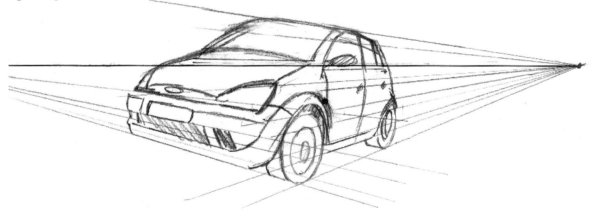

Step 3

Add the final detail. Note how blended shading provides substance, and the dark areas around the tyres and windscreen convey depth. Rub out all your temporary lines – and it's done!

◼ *Aerial Perspective*

*This type of perspective shows how objects lose their detail
and clarity as they fade into the distance.*

FLYING SAUCERS

See how the shading is much stronger when the flying saucers are in the foreground, and the outlines are lighter as the objects recede. This is due to the effect of the atmosphere. Notice also how the saucer size decreases. If objects are overlapped, like the two crafts mid-distance, this adds an impression of depth.

◼ *Foreshortening*

Foreshortening is perspective applied to a single object.

- In **Picture 1** the boy's hands are much bigger than normal in relation to his body. They are strongly foreshortened because his arms are outstretched towards us. In fact, you can hardly see his arms but the pose is believable all the same.
- In **Picture 2** we see that with foreshortening the part of the object furthest away from the viewer (the lower body) is much smaller than the part of the object nearest to the viewer (the head).

CURVES

Depending on the viewpoint, the curve of the people's clothes are curved upwards or downwards (*See* Pictures 1, 2 and 3).

Picture 1

Picture 2

Picture 3

BORDERS & REPEATING PATTERNS

Borders surrounding or adorning a page can be impressive, and look as if they have taken hours to complete! However, they often consist of repeated patterns that can be simply copied over and over again in a very short period of time.

■ *Box pattern*

Step 1

This shows the beginnings of a simple repeat pattern. Boxes are roughed out, ensuring they are all the same size and evenly spaced from each other.

Step 2

This shows the finished boxes. Note how boxes 1–4 comprise the complete sequence, which is just repeated again and again.

It is important to remember to measure up the area of the page where you want to do the border, and then measure up the size of the repeat pattern sequence. You may have to reduce or enlarge your pattern to fit the area perfectly.

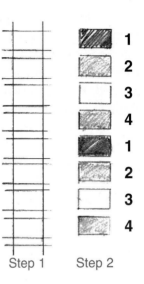

Step 1   Step 2

■ *Curve pattern*

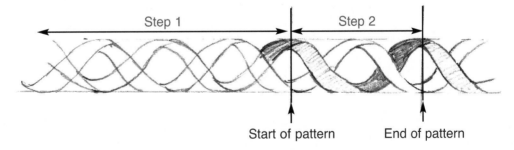

Step 1   Step 2

Start of pattern   End of pattern

Step 1

This shows how I designed this interesting double curving pattern. I drew one ribbon-like curve and then reversed it and put it on top of the other one. (**Note:** A lightbox is very handy here.)

Step 2

This shows one of the curves filled in with the overlap lines erased. Two vertical lines are inserted to show you the start and end of the pattern, which also marks where the pattern can be repeated again and again.

Flower pattern

To make the flower border:
- Trace each border section below with the aid of a lightbox.
- Estimate the correct size of each border section so they will all fit in your finished border, and reduce or enlarge on a photocopier if necessary. Then cut out each section onto separate pieces of paper.
- Put a clean sheet of paper on the lightbox (which is switched on!). With your pencil draw a temporary box frame where you want the border to be done.
- Place the top of the border section under the clean sheet in the **top left** area. Draw the image on the clean sheet of paper. Then remove the top section and turn it over so it is now reversed. Using this, now draw in the **top right** area, slightly overlapping the previous image. See the finished border pattern on the opposite page for reference.
- Using all the other sections, draw them in their correct positions, moving them around where needed. Keep referring frequently to page 59! Before you know it, your border is done!
- Redraw everything with a pen. Finally, you can erase the pencil lines and temporary frame.

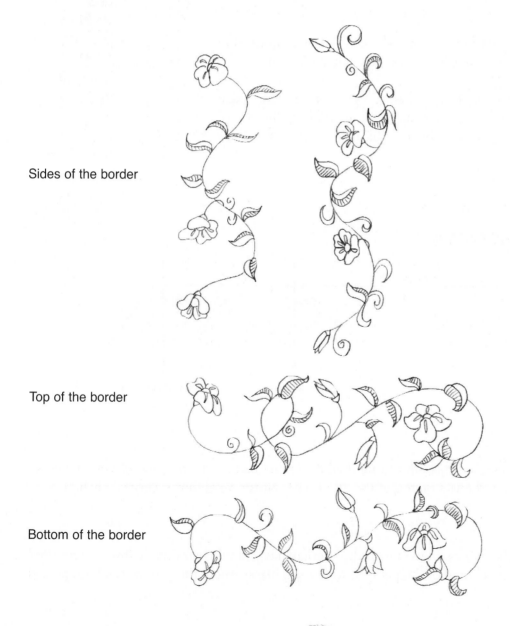

Sides of the border

Top of the border

Bottom of the border

There is a Beauty at the Goal of Life

There is a beauty at the goal of life,
A beauty growing since the world began,
Through every age and race, through lapse and
strife,
Till the great human soul complete her span.
Beneath the waves of storm that lash and burn,
The currents of blind passion that appal,
To listen and keep watch till we discern
The tide of sovereign truth that guides it all;
So to address our spirit to the height,
And so attune them to the valiant whole,
That the great light be clearer for our light,
And the great soul the stronger for our soul:
To have done this is to have lived, though fame
Remember us with no familiar name.

— Archibald Lampman

The finished flower border was painted in bright colours in the original.
Now you have a go!

USING A REFERENCE

While looking for inspiration for a cartoon depicting a shark attack I came across this photograph. It includes the image of a young girl and her friends pretending to scale a cliff face. Her pose is just what I need for a reference.

SHARK ATTACK

In the cartoon, my character is a boy but his pose is quite similar to the girl on the right of the photo.

- Drawing on my knowledge of the human figure (*See* Chapter 4), I have drawn him clinging to an outcrop of rock.
- Drips of water running off the boy tell us he has just emerged from the water, and the dashes around his head indicate surprise and fear (*See* Chapter 7).

ENDNOTE

In time, all these techniques will become second nature and you will see immediately what is needed to create a drawing the way YOU want it to be perceived. You can do it! Practise, practise, practise!

Chapter 4
The Human Figure

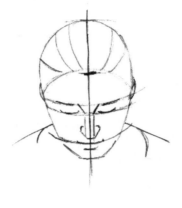 

Overview

- Knowing the correct proportions of features in the face and body, along with knowledge of basic bone and muscle construction, will enable you to draw people realistically.
- There is something special about drawing one of our own kind, and also great satisfaction when you render an accurate representation, either for yourself or others.

BODY STRUCTURE

SKELETON

■ *Profile (Side) and Body Outline*

Here is the profile of a man, showing the skeleton and overlying body structure.

Let's look at a few features:
- The head fits into the body about eight times. (See the indicator lines on the right.) This general rule varies from person to person, so when you are drawing a figure, measure the total head distance for that figure. It is a good way of getting correct distances between body areas.
- See how the neck tilts forward a little? This is part of a body's natural posture.
- Notice that the arm at rest bends forward a bit. It is not hanging straight down! And the fingers at rest curve inwards.
- See how the back is not totally straight – the spine curves slightly.
- Note where some bones in the body are close to the surface, for example the shinbone, front ribs, fingers, kneecap, and the elbow. Often the indication of these bones can provide added substance and structure when drawing and shading in a figure.

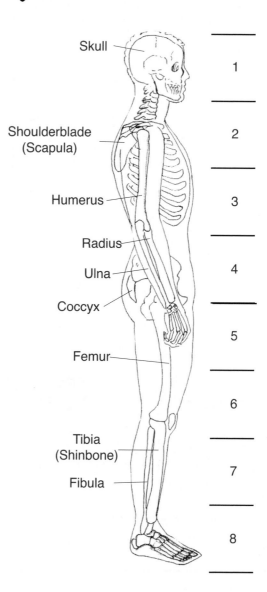

Skull

Shoulderblade (Scapula)

Humerus

Radius

Ulna

Coccyx

Femur

Tibia (Shinbone)

Fibula

1
2
3
4
5
6
7
8

Note

WOMAN'S SKELETON
A woman's skeleton differs from that of a man in that her pelvis is wider and shoulders are narrower. The bone structure overall is finer, especially around the neck, knees, wrists and ankles.

■ *Front & Body Outline* ■ *Rear & Body Outline*

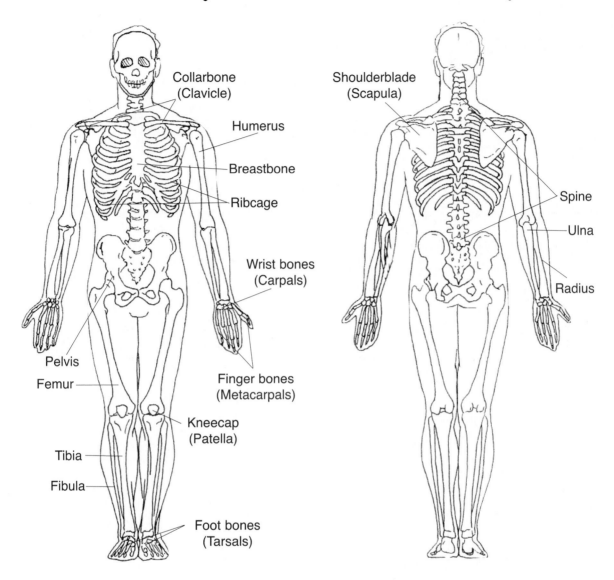

Collarbone
(Clavicle)

Humerus

Breastbone

Ribcage

Wrist bones
(Carpals)

Pelvis

Femur

Finger bones
(Metacarpals)

Kneecap
(Patella)

Tibia

Fibula

Foot bones
(Tarsals)

Shoulderblade
(Scapula)

Spine

Ulna

Radius

FRONT

- See how the femurs (thighbones) fit into the pelvis (hipbones) and how they slant down towards the patellas (kneecaps).
- See also how the tibia and fibula (lower leg bones) are arranged and how this affects the placement of the leg muscles.
- The clavicles (collarbones) are attached to the scapula (shoulderblades) and the humerus.

REAR

- Notice the length of the arms. See that the fingers (straightened here) end mid-thigh.
- When the arms are bent or rotated, the scapula can become quite prominent.

MUSCLES ON A MALE

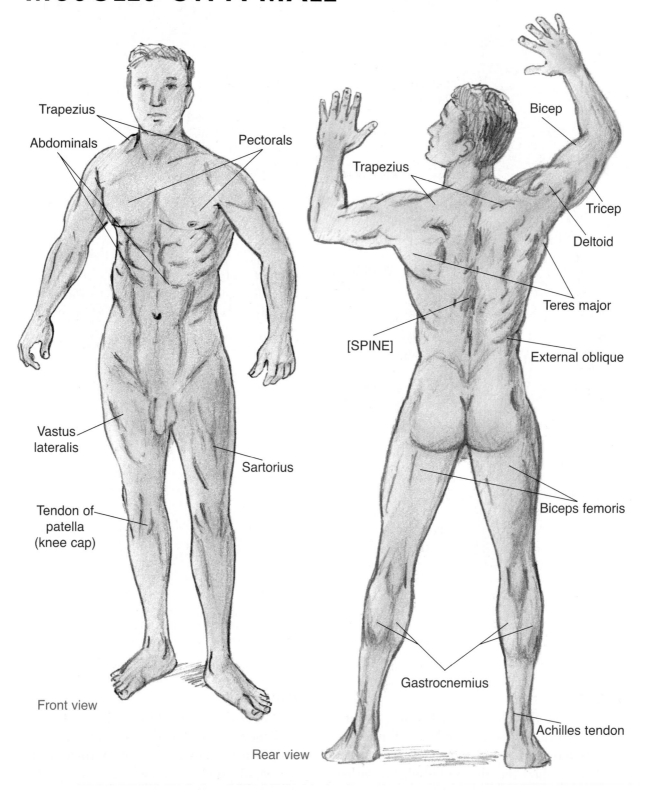

Trapezius

Abdominals

Pectorals

Bicep

Trapezius

Tricep

Deltoid

Teres major

[SPINE]

External oblique

Vastus lateralis

Sartorius

Tendon of patella (knee cap)

Biceps femoris

Front view

Gastrocnemius

Rear view

Achilles tendon

- When you are drawing a realistic representation of the human figure you may be tempted to leave out certain muscle areas – maybe you think they won't look right on your final drawing. But they will!
- To make muscle areas more visible it is very helpful to shade accordingly.
- Notice that there are two muscles side by side on the lower leg. These gastrocnemius muscles are more obvious on men than women.

MUSCLES ON A FEMALE

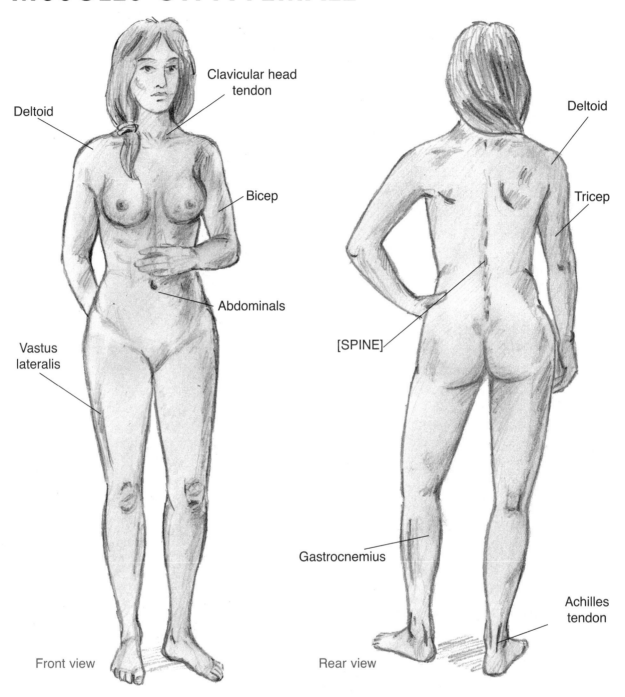

Deltoid

Clavicular head tendon

Bicep

Abdominals

Vastus lateralis

Front view

Deltoid

Tricep

[SPINE]

Gastrocnemius

Achilles tendon

Rear view

- The muscles on this female are much less obvious than on the male.
- In spite of this, the indication of muscle is still there. In the front view note the smooth curves on arms and legs, and at the abdomen. Shading has been applied to give a realistic appearance.

NOW YOUR TURN

Draw the male and female figure. Remember to measure the number of heads in the body to calculate distances between body areas. Work from photographs or pictures, or life!

■ Muscles of the Arm

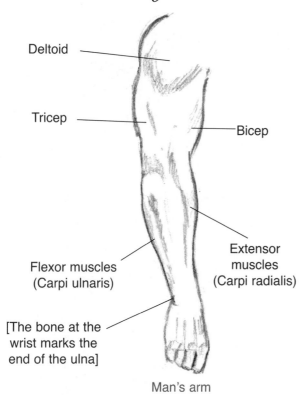

Deltoid

Tricep

Bicep

Flexor muscles
(Carpi ulnaris)

Extensor
muscles
(Carpi radialis)

[The bone at the
wrist marks the
end of the ulna]

Man's arm

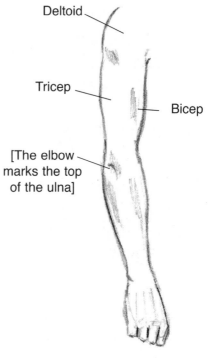

Deltoid

Tricep

Bicep

[The elbow
marks the top
of the ulna]

Woman's arm

ARM MUSCLE IN ACTION
- Extensor muscles are those that enable part of a body to stretch out. Flexor muscles are those that enable part of a body to bend. When an extensor muscle is in use the flexor is at rest, and vice versa. For example, the bicep is a flexor and the tricep is an extensor.

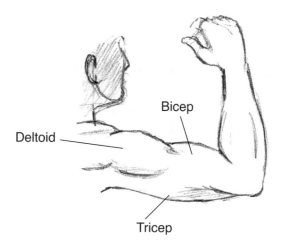

Bicep

Deltoid

Tricep

HELPFUL BODY DIMENSIONS (MAN OR WOMAN)
- The arm, from shoulder to elbow, is slightly shorter than the length of the arm from elbow to wrist.
- The leg from the top of the thigh to the knee is about the same length as from the knee to the ankle.
- The open hand is nearly the length of the face from chin to forehead. Try it and see.
- In general, the form of a female body is less defined because of subcutaneous fat which covers the muscles.

Muscles of the leg

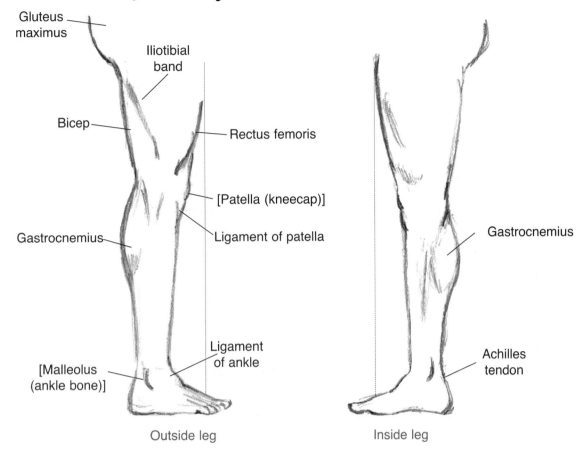

Gluteus maximus

Iliotibial band

Bicep

Rectus femoris

[Patella (kneecap)]

Gastrocnemius

Ligament of patella

Gastrocnemius

Ligament of ankle

[Malleolus (ankle bone)]

Achilles tendon

Outside leg

Inside leg

- Legs are not vertical! See the slight angle of the leg.
- See how more toes are visible on the outside leg and more of the gastrocnemius muscle is apparent on the inside leg.

Leg Bending

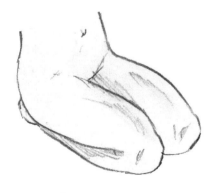

- See how the lower leg muscles are pushed out and sit under the thigh muscles.

- Notice how the upper and lower leg muscles are pressed outwards in this kneeling position. Also see there are little or no straight lines anywhere!

THE HAND

With our hands we gesture, make tools, write, and do numerous other things.

- When we look at the hand we see it is made up of four fingers, thumb, back and palm.
- The underlying bone allows the hand to be extremely flexible.
- Hands can be seen in hundreds of different positions and angles, so every time you draw them it is probably in a new position!
- Everyone's hand is different, so spend time getting the details right.
- Drawing the hand takes patience, so don't get discouraged.

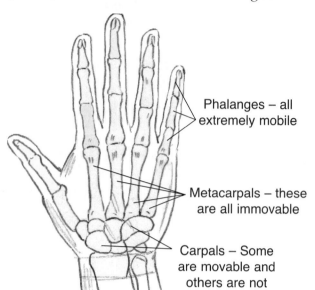

Phalanges – all extremely mobile

Metacarpals – these are all immovable

Carpals – Some are movable and others are not

Constructing an Open Hand – front

Step 1

Draw a rough square, angled at one side.

Step 2

Add lines for the fingers and thumbs, and draw in their rough shapes. Draw a curved line for the thumb muscle.

Step 3

Put in creases for the finger joints, and lines on the hand. The vertical lines show how the wrist lines up with the index and little finger.

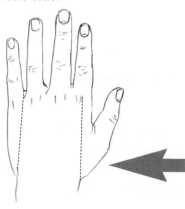

NOW YOUR TURN

Here is a finished drawing of the back of the hand. Practice drawing it in the same way as the 'front of the hand' above.

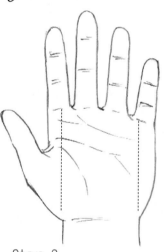

Here is a selection of male and female hands, with roughs of each one done using various methods. Try out some of these and then draw your own hand in different positions. (Remember the methods learned in Chapter 2.)

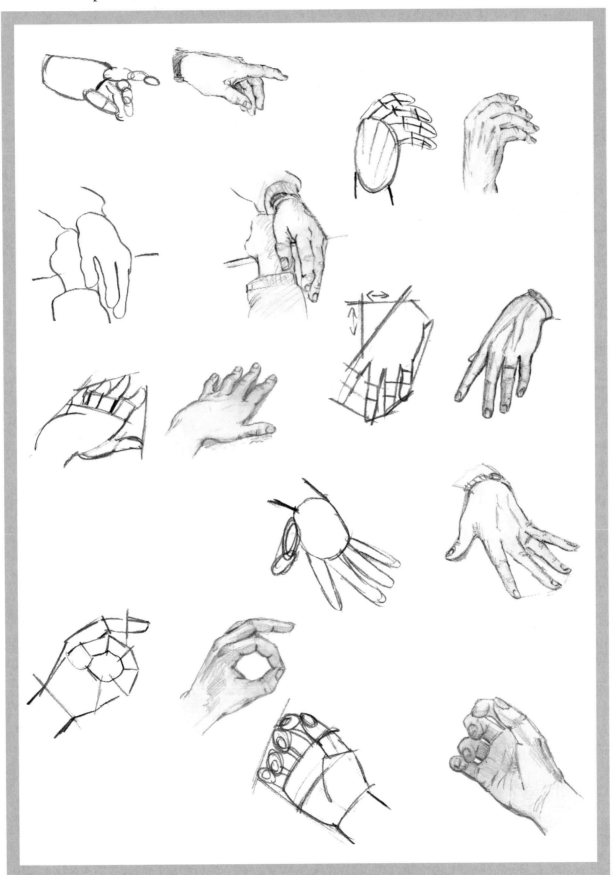

THE FOOT

Feet are primarily used to support us.

- When we look at a foot we see it is made up of five toes, with one toe considerably larger than the others!
- The diagram shows the underlying bone structure. Generally speaking the foot is not quite as flexible as the hand.
- What makes the foot point, rotate and move up, down and sideways are its muscles, ligaments and tendons.

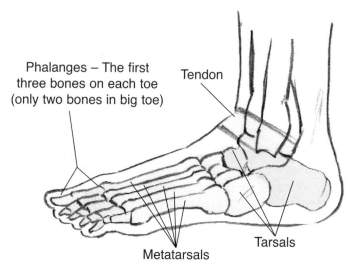

Phalanges – The first three bones on each toe (only two bones in big toe)

Tendon

Metatarsals

Tarsals

◼ *Constructing a Foot*

Remember: Draw WHAT YOU SEE and the accurate drawing will emerge.

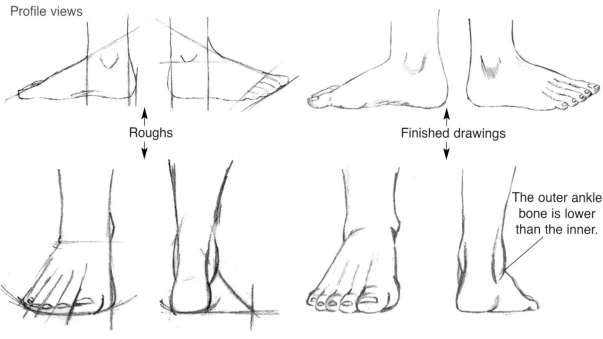

Profile views

Roughs

Finished drawings

The outer ankle bone is lower than the inner.

Front and rear views

More examples for you to try!

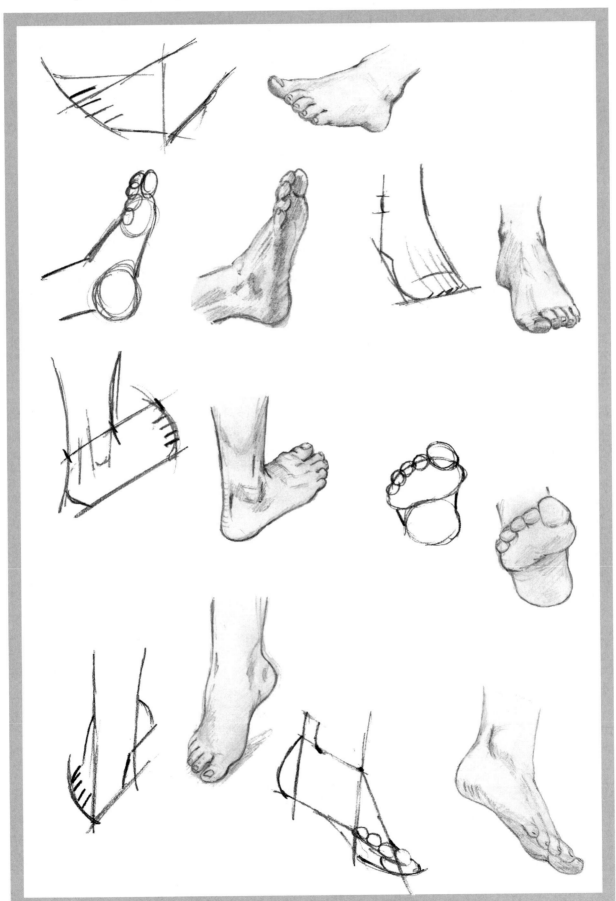

■ *Body Breakdowns*

- As people grow up and grow old, their bodies change and develop.
- This measuring chart gives an average estimation of how many heads fit into different bodies.
- A child's head is quite big in relation to its body when compared to an adult. For example, the small child's body (A) is only three and a half heads high, whereas the adult woman's body (D) is seven and a half heads high.
- When people get old (F) they shrink, and can lose a head height or more.

MEASURING CHART

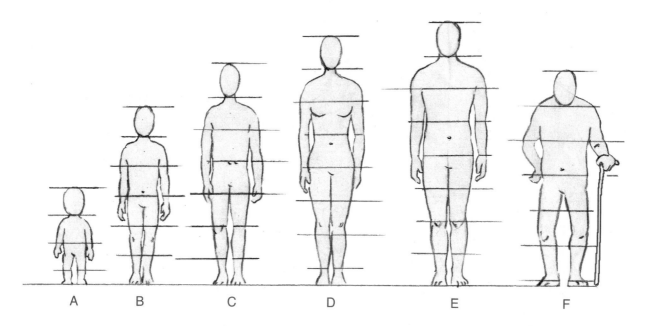

A   B   C   D   E   F

■ *Balance*

When part of the body bends in one direction the other part must bend in the opposite direction. This is to balance the body – otherwise gravity will ensure the person will fall over.

THE HEAD

Even though everyone has one set of eyes and ears, one nose and mouth, each person has their own unique facial characteristics.

■ *Basic construction of the head*

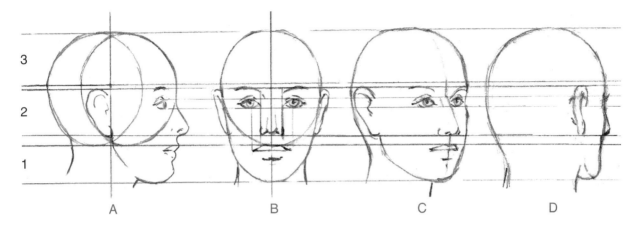

A. PROFILE
- See how the width of the skull is two circles overlapping (or you can draw the skull as an oval on its side!).
- See also where the ear is placed on the head, slightly slanted backwards.
  Note that the top of the ear is level with the eyebrow, and the bottom of the ear is level with the end of the nose.
- The head can be roughly divided into three: **1.** From the chin to the end of nose, **2.** From the end of nose to just above the eyebrows, **3.** From above the eyebrows to the top of head (a little more space here than the other two thirds).

B. FULL FACE
- The inside corner of each eye is level with the sides of the nostrils.
- When the face is in repose, the sides of the mouths line up with the pupils of the eyes.
- See how the ear shape has changed from that in profile view.

C. THREE-QUARTER FRONT
- See how the mouth and eye on the far side of the face are distorted and condensed.
- The cheekbone on the far side is clearly defined.
- The far nostril is barely visible.
- Three-quarter view portraits are very popular, as they are interesting to draw and are pleasing to look at.
- See how the ear shape has changed again.

D. THREE-QUARTER BACK
- Very little is seen of the face – just an eyelash and part of the eyebrow, and a small area of the nose.
- The ear shape has changed once more.

Facial Differences between Men and Women

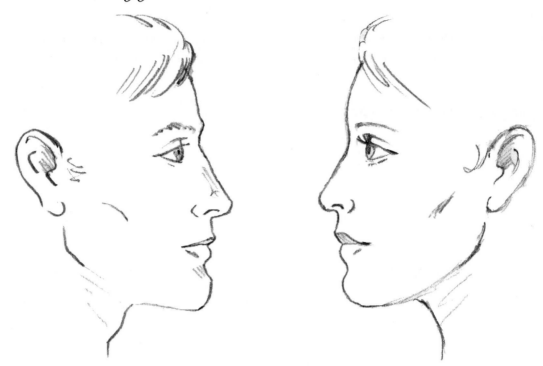

- The female face is softer in appearance than the male face.
- The chin is stronger and more defined in the male.
- The nose is more rounded in the female.
- Lips in general are thinner in the male.
- On the neck, a man has an Adam's apple, and a woman has just a tiny indication of one.

The Neck

In general, a man's neck is thicker than a woman's.

- The top picture is an inaccurate drawing. The neck does not meet the shoulders like this – straight down and across!
- The bottom drawing shows that the neck meets the **trapezius** muscles on the way down. Only then are the shoulders drawn.
- Also note the **clavicular head tendons**. They are not so prominent when the head is facing directly forward. When the head is tilted upwards, they are much more apparent. The collarbone may also be seen.

Everyone has a different neck shape, so bear this in mind when drawing from observation.

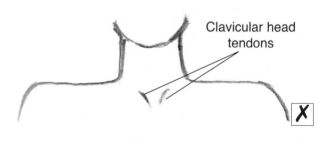

Clavicular head tendons

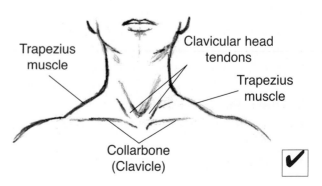

Trapezius muscle

Clavicular head tendons

Trapezius muscle

Collarbone (Clavicle)

Looking Up and Down

A. LOOKING UP – THREE-QUARTER VIEW

- See how the features change as the face is tilted up.
- Note that the far eye is quite distorted.
- When drawing the jawline just shade it lightly – no strong lines are needed here.
- Since the light source is usually from above, and the upper lip curves inwards, shade it darker than the lower lip.

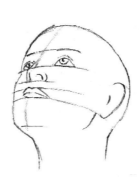 

Ⓐ

B. LOOKING UP – FRONT VIEW

- Again, see how the eyes are distorted and on line with the tip of the nose.
- Also note the flattened irises.
- In the rough the ears look strange! But in the final drawing you can see they look fine.

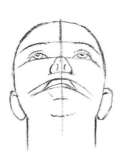 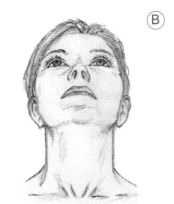

Ⓑ

C. LOOKING DOWN – THREE-QUARTER VIEW

- Always remember to line up the eyes and eyebrows as shown in the rough.
- Note again how the ears change position – this time they are shifted up to eye level.
- Less of the top lip is visible now.
- Also note how high the shoulders are placed.

Ⓒ

D. LOOKING DOWN – FRONT VIEW

- The shoulders are on line with the upper cheekbones.
- See that the tip of the nose is just above the lip and the nostrils are higher than the tip of the nose.
- In the rough, notice the curves of the lines on the face and the curves in the hair lines, compared with the final drawing.

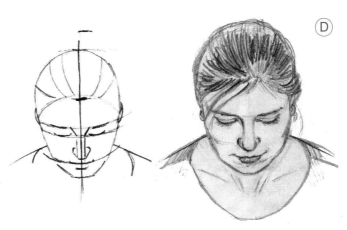

Ⓓ

THE EYE

Eyes are called the windows of the soul, as they convey emotions and expression that often go beyond words. When we look at or talk to someone it is usually their eyes we look at first.

Look at the eye on the right. This is NOT how an eye should be drawn. The shape should not be a perfect oval. When the iris circle touches the top and bottom of the eye like this, it gives the eye a surprised look. But we don't always look surprised!

HOW AN EYE IS DRAWN

Step 1 | Step 2 | Step 3 | Step 4

Step 1

Draw an oval.

Step 2

Draw a line through the middle of the oval. Raise the left corner of the oval a little and add a tear duct below the right corner.

Step 3

Add the iris and pupil. See that the top of the iris is hidden, leaving space at the bottom of the eye.

Add a highlight to the eye.

Step 4

Put in the eyelid, upper eyelashes and smaller lower lashes.

Add some shading, making the upper eye area darker.

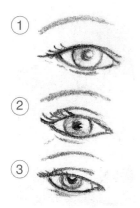

EXAMPLES OF DIFFERENT EYELIDS
- The first eye has an eyelid that is hardly seen.
- The second eye has an eyelid that is clearly visible.
- The third eye is almond shaped. The eyelid is seen, and conforms to the shape of the eye.

EXAMPLES OF DIFFERENT EYEBROWS
- The first set of eyebrows are very low near the eyes.
- The second set has eyebrows that slant upwards.
- The third set of eyebrows slant downwards.
- The fourth set are thick and bushy.

Eyes – front view

When you are drawing eyes from a front view, try to keep them exactly level with each other. It helps if you draw a temporary horizontal line across both eyes.

Picture 1 shows eyes with a normal gaze.
- Note the heavy eyelids on this person.
- The lower parts of these eyes dip down slightly more than normal.

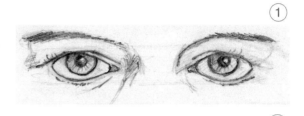

Picture 2 shows angry eyes.
- See how the eyebrows nearly meet the eyes.
- The folds of the eyelids slant up and partially cover the top of the eyes.
- Two vertical lines are seen between the eyes.

Picture 3 shows laughing eyes.
- Notice how only the mid-section of the irises are now seen.
- The cheek muscles push up the fatty tissue under the eyes.
- Creases at the side of the eyes are visible.

Eye – profile

- The iris is not a circle any more; it is more disc-shaped. And the pupil does not extend to the very front of the eye.

Eyes – three-quarter profile

- The eyes of this young person are at an angle. See how both eyes are slightly distorted as they look past us.
- You can only see about half of the far eye because the nose is blocking the rest of it.

Young person

- The eyes of this older person are not at an angle.
- Notice the darkish ridge at the top of the eyelid. The fat around the eyes is no longer there so the features of muscle and bone are more apparent.

Old person

Hot Tip

When drawing front view, the distance between eyes is the width of one eye. Test it and see!

THE MOUTH

*The mouth (lips, teeth, tongue) is the most movable area on the face,
and through which we talk and eat. Men's lips in general are thinner than women's
and the older you get the thinner your lips become.*

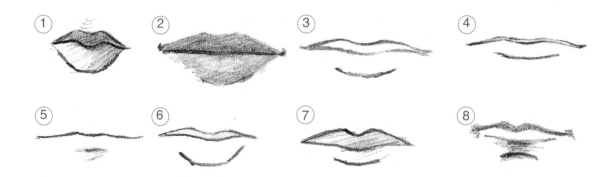

1. POUTY LIPS. See how the upper lip is comprised of two upside-down W's.
   Also notice how the upper lip is darker than the lower because less light falls
   on it.
2. FULL LIPS. These are shaded with no outlines. This upper lip has an outer
   upside-down W shape and an inner straight line.
3. OUTLINE OF LIPS. See how the lower lip need not be completely finished.
4. THIN LIPS. Just an indication is given of an upper lip.
5. VERY THIN LIPS! No upper lip is visible, and the lower lip is shown as a soft line.
6. See that the lower lip is a good deal bigger here.
7. In contrast, here the upper lip is larger.
8. THIN LIPS AGAIN. The upper part of a strong chin is seen.

▉ *Open Mouth – front view*

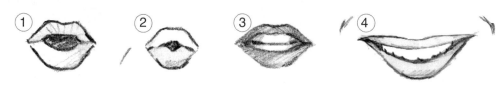

1. Lips making an 'oh' sound.
2. Lips saying 'ooooo!'
3. Lips speaking the consonants: C, D, S or T!
4. Lips smiling. **Note:** Each tooth (unless very close up) does not have to be completely drawn.

THE NOSE

Noses come in all shapes and sizes. Some types are quite distinctive and are given names: button nose, Roman nose, snub nose, pug nose!

■ *Profile*

- See the varying shapes.

■ *Three-quarter view*

- Depending on the angle, a greater or lesser part of the far nostril can be seen.
- You can use a solid line or shading for the front of the nose – whichever seems most suitable.

■ *Front view*

- Notice how lines can be connected using shading.

THE EAR

There are hundreds of different types of ears. We often do not notice this because we are concentrating more on a person's face!

① 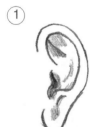 ② 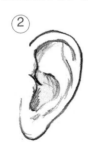 ③ 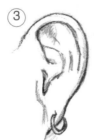 ④  ⑤

⑥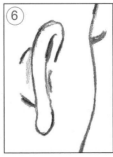

- Nos. 1, 2 and 3 show differently shaped ears in profile.
- No. 4 shows an ear the way it would appear when you see a person in three-quarter profile.
- No. 5 is how you see an ear when looking at someone full front view.
- No. 6 is the view from three-quarter rear, with the outline of the face added.

PORTRAITS

*Take as much time as you need and make as many changes
and roughs as you want as you develop the drawings below.*

■ *Using rounded shapes and measuring*

WINDSWEPT CHILD

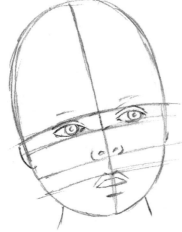

Step 1

The first drawing shows a rough oval for the head. Lines have
been drawn to indicate nose, eyes and mouth.

Notice that the eyes are about halfway down the head.

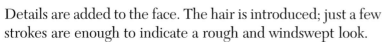

Step 2

Details are added to the face. The hair is introduced; just a few
strokes are enough to indicate a rough and windswept look.

The outline of the jersey is drawn and shading is introduced
to the eyes and mouth.

Step 3

More shading is added
and any temporary lines
are removed.

Step 4

The final drawing shows further development of shading
which enhances the poignant feel of the young boy's face.

SMILING BABY
You can draw a tot's face
in a few simple steps.

Step 1

- The head is drawn as a rough oval.
- The slightly curved vertical line shows that the face is slightly off-centre.
- Lines for the eyes, nose and mouth are added.
- A very rough indication is shown for the ears and hair. (Artistic license has been applied to add a neck!)

Step 2

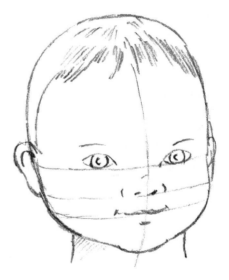

- The baby's face shape is developed: detail is begun on the hair, and the eyes and ears are given more defined shape.
- A light shadow is drawn on the neck.

Step 3

- The finished drawing retains a simplicity while showing all the features of the baby's face.
- Rough strokes are applied to indicate more hair on the baby's head. Shading has been added to the ears and neck, and detail is given to the eyes, remembering to add highlights!

■ *Using measuring and scribbling*

*Here is another portrait drawn from a photograph.
Remember to check angles again and again as you progress!*

Indicator lines

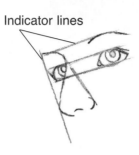

LATIN BEAUTY

Step 1

Lightly draw indicator lines for the positioning of eyes and eyebrows, and then draw them in.

Find where the nostril is positioned by drawing a line from the bridge of the nose down.

Draw a line on the left of the face to get the correct angle of the face, and to see where the tip of the nose is.

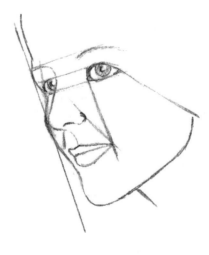

Step 2

Extend the line from the tip of the nose downwards. This helps you to see how far in from this line the chin and mouth are. Then draw the mouth. Note the indicator line drawn from the eye to the mouth in order to find the correct position of the end of the mouth.

Draw another line from the eye to the jawline. Add in the rest of the shape of the face, drawing more indicator lines if you need them.

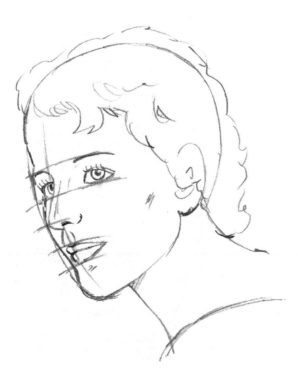

Step 3

Develop the features, checking you are putting everything in the correct place.

Now draw the shape of the head and rough out the hair.

Step 4

Begin to rub out the indicator lines (or redraw your sketch using a lightbox!).

Add detail to the hair and face. Draw the outline of the blouse.

Draw strokes for the hair following their natural wave.

Shading may also be started. Remember to shade the upper lip slightly darker.

Step 5

The final stage: Use a softer pencil to develop shading, and keep looking back and forth at the original photograph to check your progress. You can blend with your finger if you like.

Remember to add highlights to the eyes so they appear alive.

Don't draw the blouse too dark as it would take attention away from the face.

Notice that the light source is from the left.

Hot Tip

The often-used term Chiaroscuro means the balance of light and shadow in a picture, most popularly traced back to Italian painter Caravaggio, where this process can be clearly seen.

Using measuring and scribbling

LAUGHING MAN

See how I used artistic license: I removed his hand from his face, added the top of his head and changed his expression a little!

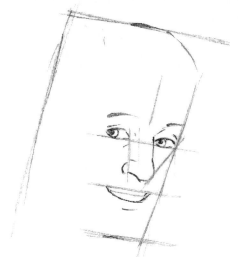

Step 1

As before, draw the eyes first. From there, draw lines to find where the nose and mouth are situated.

Add more lines to show the overall head and face shape.

Step 2

Develop the features, remembering the curves of the face. See how the man's cheeks are pushed up as he laughs. Add the outline for a moustache.

Step 3

Laughter lines should be prominent at the corner of his eyes. Don't forget to add the wrinkles on his forehead and bags under his eyes.

Draw a few curved lines for his hair and develop the moustache further.

Step 4

The finished picture, showing added shading and further detail.

GALLERY

*Armed with all your new information about how the body works,
you can approach drawing the human figure with greater confidence.*

- The first thing to do is check that the figure you want to draw will fit on your paper and whether it is better to draw on a longer or wider sheet.
- When you are drawing a person either from a picture or from life, sometimes give yourself a time limit. This can make you concentrate and focus better.
- If you feel you are not getting a body shape right, leave that drawing and start on a new pose. Go back to your unfinished drawing later and work on the areas you found difficult. By constantly correcting your weak areas in this way you refine and improve your drawing abilities.
- I find it easier to start drawing a figure at the head, but see what suits yourself! And don't worry about getting the facial features accurate – with figure sketches it is the overall body you are more concerned with.
- Again, it is up to you to tidy up your sketches or leave them in a rough style.

STANDING MAN
This was done quite fast, with attention mainly paid to accuracy of the body shape.

WOMAN READING
This is a more finished drawing. Care was taken with her posture and the surrounding props.

NOW YOUR TURN

Ask your model to give you five poses at one minute each, three poses at three minutes each, one pose for five minutes and one pose for ten minutes.

Vary these exercises and enjoy the process. Remember, time limits can help you to focus more, and so produce more accurate drawings.

SEATED MAN

The intention here was to get as accurate a drawing as possible in a very short time. See how the head tilts forwards here as he cups his hands behind his neck.

Note the foreshortening at the near elbow and near knee. This is one of those times to draw what you SEE and not what you THINK you see.

Foreshortening
See page 56

SEATED WOMAN

This was done with strong lines, which give the figure a sense of immediacy and vitality. 4B pencil was used for the outline and hair.

Notice the light shading on the body.

CARTWHEEL

This girl was drawn from a photograph. The advantage of photos is that they capture movements which could be otherwise difficult to reproduce accurately.

Notice how the top of the feet are a little blurred to show motion. A few speed lines were added too.

MATURE WOMAN

I took time with this life sketch. Note the posture of the body – it is quite relaxed. See how the upper back slopes, and notice the forward angle of the neck and head.

Shading was added, but not too strongly – a B pencil in this case.

ENDNOTE

Experimentation and practice improves and enhances your accuracy in drawing the human figure. Attend a life drawing class, ask friends to pose for you, and draw from photographs or sculptures in art galleries. Vary your artwork.

Chapter 5
Animals

Overview

The world of animals is extremely diverse! Since there is little chance of covering every animal in this chapter, you will be shown examples of some well-known species instead. Guidelines for dogs, cats, birds and dolphins will help you to draw many other types of animals. The following aids are given:
*   Profile skeletons so you understand structures,
*   Labelled diagrams of body parts,
*   Working examples of some of the Essential Methods to demonstrate different ways of drawing animals,
*   Common mistakes with some species so you know what to avoid!

DOGS

There are many types of dogs today, due to selective breeding and cross-breeding throughout the centuries. All domestic dogs are descended from the wolf.

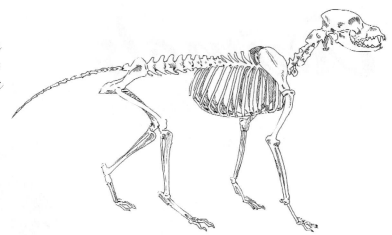

A Closer Look

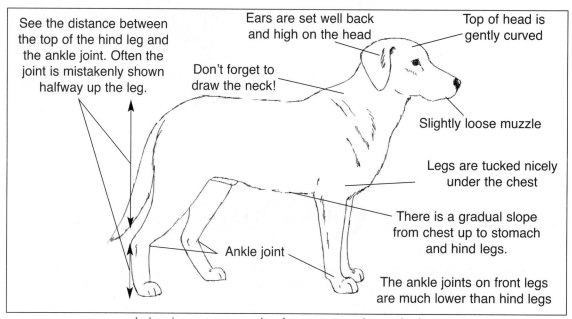

See the distance between the top of the hind leg and the ankle joint. Often the joint is mistakenly shown halfway up the leg.

Ears are set well back and high on the head

Top of head is gently curved

Don't forget to draw the neck!

Slightly loose muzzle

Legs are tucked nicely under the chest

There is a gradual slope from chest up to stomach and hind legs.

Ankle joint

The ankle joints on front legs are much lower than hind legs

Labrador – an example of an average domestic dog

Shape

Here is an example of the rounded shapes method used to get an outline of the labrador.

When you are happy with your shape, then bring in the detail as seen in the drawing above. Don't be afraid to change and alter as necessary.

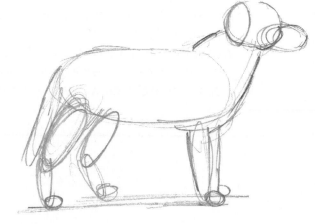

■ *Common Mistakes*

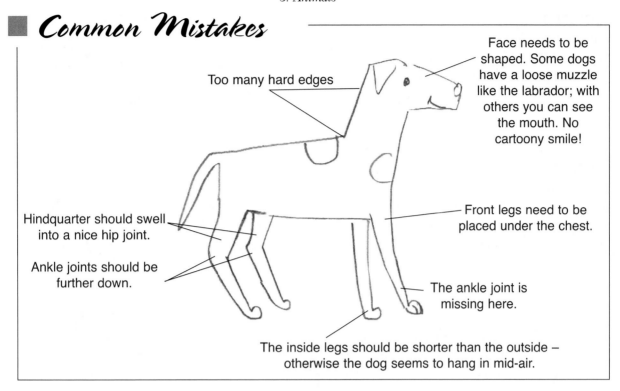

Too many hard edges

Face needs to be shaped. Some dogs have a loose muzzle like the labrador; with others you can see the mouth. No cartoony smile!

Hindquarter should swell into a nice hip joint.

Ankle joints should be further down.

Front legs need to be placed under the chest.

The ankle joint is missing here.

The inside legs should be shorter than the outside – otherwise the dog seems to hang in mid-air.

■ *Heads*

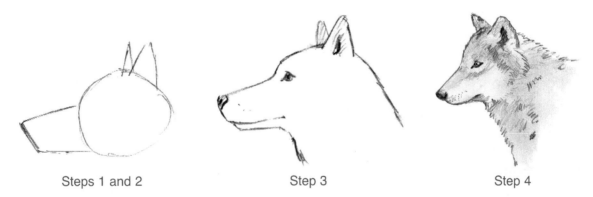

| Steps 1 and 2 | Step 3 | Step 4 |

Step 1 and 2

To draw a dog in profile, first draw a rough circle.
Carefully note how far down from the head the beginning of the muzzle begins, and also see where the ears are on the head.

Step 3

Smooth the hard-edged lines and add the eye and other details. Notice that the mouth line ends directly below the beginning of the eye.

Step 4

To achieve a 'wolf' look, just sharpen the muzzle area, widen the head and add extra fur. Add shading.

PICTURE 1

This is the front view of a Pekingese. See how the little nose being placed close to the eyes emphasises the effect of a flat face.

PICTURE 2

This is the profile of a dog known as the Japanese Chin. The button nose is placed right in front of the eyes, and the muzzle is just a gentle swelling below.

PICTURE 3

Here we have a three-quarter view of a boxer. Note that its strong jaw juts out further than the nose, and the eye is well set back and upwards from the nose.

The above descriptions should help you to be aware of different features when drawing various dog faces.

Hot Tip

DRAWING FUR

You know how you can draw a tick (✔) when marking something as correct?
- Diagram A shows this effect when drawing long or short fur – a heavy start with the pencil flicking and then tapering off. This technique is used a lot in drawing fur.
- Diagram B is for shorter fur.
- Diagram C is wavy fur, also using the 'tick' effect.

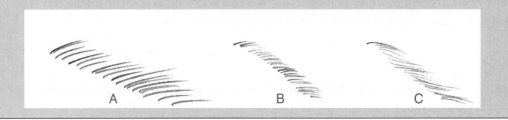

Domestic Dog Bodies

LABRADOR

In this drawing see how parts of the body are **foreshortened**. The rough has been done as a contour drawing, and then modified to produce the finished drawing.

See how length of muzzle is indicated by drawing a short line between the eye and nose.

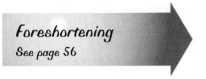

Foreshortening
See page 56

DACHSHUND

This dachshund is the longhaired version. The rough here is done by the rounded shapes method.

Also check: If you use finger measuring, you will see the body is about three heads long.

BORZOI

The borzoi has long flowing fur and elongated features. Take note of the ankle joint on front far leg and how the front foreleg slightly overlaps the hind legs as it runs.

The body has been done by finger measuring, and rounded shapes for the head. You can see from the measuring gauge on the rough that the body is about three and a half heads long.

Wild Dog Bodies

THE AFRICAN WILD DOG

This dog has a lean athletic body. Its fur is very short as it lives in a hot climate.

Finger measuring is used for the rough, along with scribbling. See how the front foreleg position was changed.

Final detail and strong shading are added. Fur strokes are only really necessary on the tail.

ARCTIC FOX

This fox has a small compact body, with long thick fur as protection against bitter cold.

The rough is done using the rounded shapes method.

Final detail is added. Most of the lines are fur strokes except for the muzzle, eyes, nose and foot. Make sure your fur strokes follow the contours of the body.

HOWLING WOLF

This howling wolf has a sturdy and powerful body, covered in dense fur. Wolves do not need to open their mouths wide to howl!

Draw this wolf, creating your own rough using one of the methods already mentioned. Notice how as the head leans back, the ears flatten.

CATS

The size of domestic and wild cats has a much greater range than domestic and wild dogs. However, there is not as much diversity within domestic cats as there is among domestic dogs.

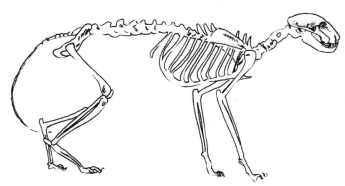

The skeleton of the cat shown here is also the basic structure for lions and tigers: a lithe sinewy body with an extremely flexible spine.

■ A Closer Look

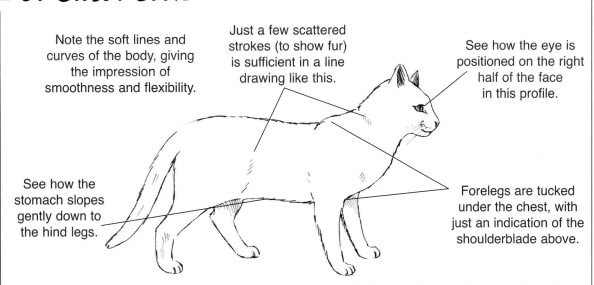

Note the soft lines and curves of the body, giving the impression of smoothness and flexibility.

Just a few scattered strokes (to show fur) is sufficient in a line drawing like this.

See how the eye is positioned on the right half of the face in this profile.

See how the stomach slopes gently down to the hind legs.

Forelegs are tucked under the chest, with just an indication of the shoulderblade above.

Shorthaired white – an example of the average domestic cat

■ Shape

Use an oval for the head. See how almost every other body part can be drawn as rounded shapes.

After finishing these areas, add lines at the neck and legs to connect the rounded shapes.

Gradually bring in the detail seen in the drawing above.

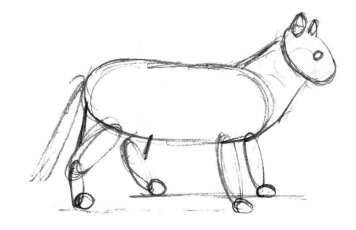

■ *Common Mistakes*

A cat face is often drawn head-on like this – much like a cartoon human face except for the line attaching nose and mouth!

The tail is just a thin line.

Legs are often drawn all the same length and without paws resulting in no perspective and no realism.

The front legs need to be positioned under the chest.

■ *Heads*

BRITISH-TYPE CAT – FULL FACE

Step 1

- Draw Circle A, and then Circle B overlapping the bottom of Circle A.
- Lightly draw temporary horizontal and vertical lines halfway across and down the face.
- Draw the eyes as slightly slanted ovals. Make sure they are the same height as each other and slightly more than an eye distance apart.
- See where there is another smaller horizontal line halfway across Circle B? This is an indicator line for the end of the nose.

Step 2

- Now add ears, taking note of their triangular shape and that they are slightly angled either side of the head.
- Add detail and shading on the ears and in the eyes.

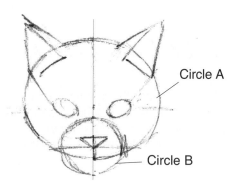

Circle A

Circle B

FOREIGN-TYPE CAT – PROFILE

The rough shows how the face is made up of an oval and semi-circle for the muzzle. The ears are triangles and the line crossing the eye will be in line with the nose.

The final drawing shows a slender elegant profile. The eyes are slightly almond-shaped.

PERSIAN CAT – THREE-QUARTER PROFILE

To get a flat look to the face, draw the nose very close to the eyes and mouth.

The head is high and flat with small ears set wide apart.

CHEETAH – THREE-QUARTER PROFILE

Use a large circle for the head and smaller circle for the muzzle.

The cheetah has the rounded features of a domestic cat, but the finished drawing shows the big cat's distinctive tear markings from eyes to mouth.

LIONESS – THREE-QUARTER PROFILE

The measuring line in the rough is a vertical line drawn upwards from the neck, which shows the positioning of the mouth and the far eye. Note also the long face, in comparison with other cat faces.

Domestic Cat Bodies

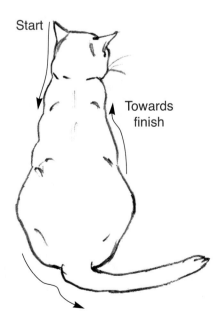

Start

Towards finish

CONTOUR DRAWING

By contour drawing a simple outline, a realistic rear view of a cat emerges. Try it yourself! If you wish, glance at your drawing now and again to make sure you are proceeding correctly.

I find it easier to draw from the head down, around the tail and back up, but judge for yourself which way you like best.

Contour drawing
See page 13

SIAMESE – FULL BODY

- The Siamese, a foreign-type cat, is much slimmer and more fine-boned than the British-type cat. Note that the face is triangle-shaped, with large wide ears, and the feet are small and dainty.
- See in the rough how the head shape has been used to find body length, denoted by circles. Indicator lines are also used to judge angles of the front and rear legs in relation to the body.
- Draw finer strokes for the fur, noting that there are more definite hard lines than soft curves on this cat.

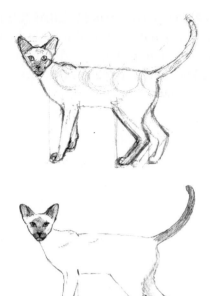

PERSIAN – FULL BODY

- The long-haired Persian has a sturdy body, short legs and bushy tail. In the rough, note how the body is formed by rounded shapes, and also see the measuring lines on the face.
- In the finished drawing elongated fur strokes to the body creates the impression of long silky fur.

MANX – FULL BODY

- The Manx cat is famous for the absence of a tail. It also has larger hindquarters than the average cat.
- Note that the indicator lines in the rough show the length of the back of the cat is two and a half heads long.

Note:
Generally wild cats are larger than their domestic cousins.

Wild Cat Bodies

TIGER – FULL BODY

- The rough is done by contour drawing.
- Things to note are: how far below the shoulderblades the head lies in this foreshortened view; and although the rear hind leg is hardly visible, it is essential to the drawing.
- Remember to draw the stripes around the body's natural curves. The drawing is finished by adding shading and detail.

LIONESS – FULL BODY

- The rough of this lioness walking away was contour drawn first. Always go for the easiest area to draw first!
- The finger measuring method is used to check the height of the ears against the back, then the distance between the forelegs and the back legs.
- Shading is finally introduced, blending with the finger.

LION – HEAD AND SHOULDERS

- A lion's mane is simply longer fur on its face! In the rough, a light outer circle marks where the mane extends around the face. Then face details are added, measuring to make sure proportions are correct.
- Note that some fur strokes are straight and others curved. The light source is from the left, so we need to lightly shade the right.

NOW YOUR TURN

As an exercise, draw the lion shown at the start of this chapter from your own rough.

BIRDS

*Over 8,500 species of birds
populate the skies today.*

All birds, from the ostrich to the wren, have the same basic structure as shown here. 'Arms' are wings for flight in nearly all birds. Their body, except for the bill and legs, is covered in feathers. The two scaly legs end in feet that usually have three toes in front and one behind. Each toe has claws.

◼ *A Closer Look*

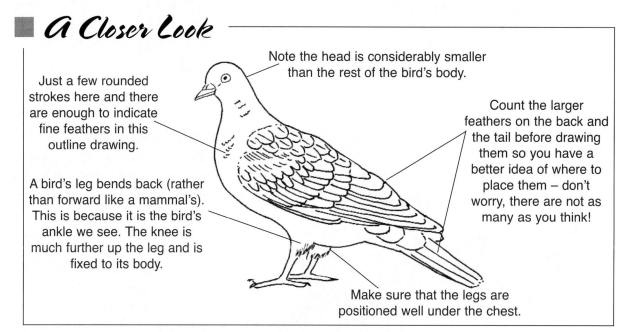

Note the head is considerably smaller than the rest of the bird's body.

Just a few rounded strokes here and there are enough to indicate fine feathers in this outline drawing.

Count the larger feathers on the back and the tail before drawing them so you have a better idea of where to place them – don't worry, there are not as many as you think!

A bird's leg bends back (rather than forward like a mammal's). This is because it is the bird's ankle we see. The knee is much further up the leg and is fixed to its body.

Make sure that the legs are positioned well under the chest.

Rock dove – an example of the average bird

ROCK DOVE

Step 1

The bird is roughed out using both rounded shapes and measuring. See the line drawn from the end of the neck downwards to get the correct positioning of the leg.

Step 2

Shading and final details are added.

Common Mistakes

The shape of the wings is wrong, and also where they should connect to the body.

The head is drawn larger than it should be.

The straight legs drawn here certainly do not look realistic! Check out other bird drawings in this chapter for feet positioning.

Types of Birds

GREAT TIT

Other common birds like robins and sparrows have the same kind of small compact body. They seem to have no neck, a fairly short straight beak and slender legs.

See that the eye is nearly on the same level as the beak, the head is a broad oval, and the body a large flattened oval. Notice where the legs are in relation to the underside of the body.

Hot Tip

DRAWING WITH FEELING!
As drawing becomes easier, now and again allow yourself to 'lose' yourself in the subject you are drawing. As an example, draw the Great Tit above, and as you do imagine how it would feel as it sits on its perch OR infuse the drawing with the feelings you are experiencing at that moment. Do you now lean heavier or lighter with your pencil on certain parts of the bird? Do you concentrate less on getting each tiny area correct and instead 'flow' with the drawing?

Check out some famous artists such as Van Gogh, Botticelli and Chagall and see how their emotions show through in their pictures. As Leonardo said, if approached in the right way, a picture can become 'silent poetry'.

RHEA

This is one of the tallest birds, and it is also flightless. The rough drawing is done by measuring and rounded shapes.

Note the lines drawn to determine where the head and beak are in relation to the neck, and the angle of the front leg.

TEAL

This duck is in its favourite location. Take note of the round head, small eyes and the placement of the beak.

Step 1

The body is roughed out using rounded shapes, taking note of the eye position.

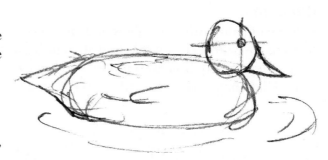

Step 2

The rough is now developed using air measuring.

When drawing the feathers, you do not have to draw every one – an impression can do just fine, as shown here on the main body area.

Step 3

This is the finished teal. See the movement and slight reflection in the water. Just a couple of curving lines can indicate motion. The reflection of a few tail feathers adds a realistic effect to the drawing.

■ *Wing Shapes*

1. WINGS FOR FAST TAKE-OFF AND TO AVOID PREDATORS

Note: All the drawings of birds in flight were done from photographs.

CHAFFINCH

The chaffinch has broad rounded wings for speedy acceleration and good steering. Birds with similar wing shapes are owls, pheasants, grouse as well as woodland birds such as sparrows and warblers.

Finger measuring was used to produce the rough and the wing feathers were counted before being drawn in.

TAWNY OWL

The shape is developed using rounded shapes and finger measuring. The banding on the wings can be done by following a natural curve of your hand as you move your pencil without your hand leaving the paper. Try it and see! These curved lines help to identify the positioning of the wings as well as the feather designs.

Shading and final feather designs are added to complete the drawing.

2. WINGS FOR SPEED AND LONG FLIGHTS

BARN SWALLOW

The barn swallow has slender curved wings adapted for continuous use. Birds with similar wing shapes are swifts, many geese, kingfishers and some predatory birds.

A rough of the bird was done using finger measuring, and finished by adding detail and shading on the wings and body.

3. WINGS FOR SOARING, GLIDING AND HOVERING

SKIMMER

The skimmer has narrow pointed wings to enable it to glide on air currents. Birds with similar wing shapes are other gulls, condors, and some birds of prey, such as the buzzard and the kestrel.

This rough has been drawn using finger measuring.

◼ *Beaks*

Some beaks are tricky to draw, like those of parrots or birds of prey.

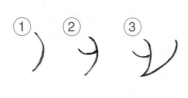 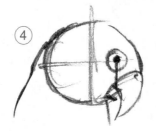 

Follow these easy steps:
1. Draw the lower part of upper beak.
2. Then draw the connecting lower beak.
3. Add in the upper part of beak.
4. Draw the head, neck and eye.
5. Finally, add shading and detail.

Modify the way you do these simple steps when you draw different types of birds. Try this golden eagle!

Golden Eagle

DOLPHINS

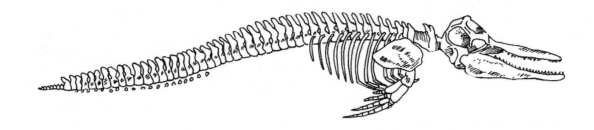

Sea mammals are different from fish in that they bear live young that suckle from their mother. Dolphins and whales are considered extremely intelligent and communicate with each other by emitting underwater sounds that travel great distances.

Dolphins have streamlined bodies perfectly adapted for the ocean, so when you are drawing them accentuate their strong curvy lines.

Note that their horizontal tail fluke, which replaces the missing hind limbs, immediately identifies them from fish. Other sea mammals such as seals and sealions have modified hind limbs in the form of flippers.

■ *A Closer Look*

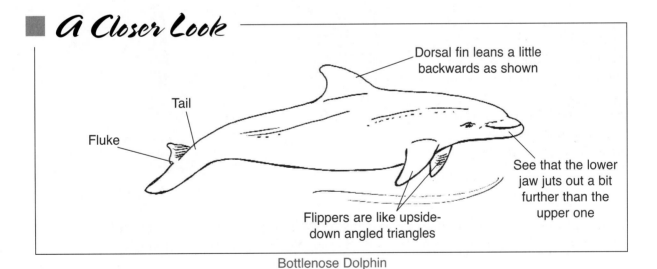

Dorsal fin leans a little backwards as shown

Tail

Fluke

See that the lower jaw juts out a bit further than the upper one

Flippers are like upside-down angled triangles

Bottlenose Dolphin

WHITESIDED DOLPHIN
These contour drawings show the dolphins in mid-leap from the sea.
Practise your own contour drawing by copying them!

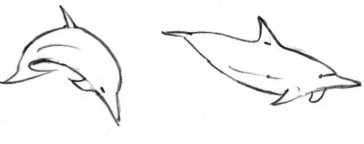

BOTTLENOSE DOLPHIN

Step 1

Use a rounded oblong shape to create the rough of the body. Flippers, fins, tail and the face area are then added.

Step 2

This is the finished bottlenose dolphin. See how the careful blending and shading creates a soft silky look to its skin.

PLAYFUL DOLPHINS

Step 1

The rough was drawn using finger measuring. Care was taken to get the correct distances and positions of the mouth and flippers. See how the eye is just at the end of the mouth line. To get correct body size, measure the head and see how many times it goes into the body.

Step 2

Note that you do not have to draw great detail on the sea splash to get a good effect. Make the foam edges slightly rounded and add shading for the darker sea tone.

ENDNOTE

Draw animals in action, at rest and interacting with each other. Feel free to start drawing from photographs, so you can draw a creature that does not move around all the time! However, if you have a pet, draw it from observation as much as you can as this exercises your visual memory as well as improving your ability.

Chapter 6
Nature

Overview

- The natural world has long been an inspiration for artists, because of its beauty and variety. Nature is all around us: in cities and towns, you will find trees, shrubs and flowers on streets, roads and in parks; in suburbia, you can choose from many types of gardens, and of course if you are lucky enough to live in the country you just have to step outside your front door.
- And when you draw nature from observation rather than a picture or photo, you will produce a drawing that seems more immediate, realistic and alive. Moreover, it is also extremely therapeutic and relaxing to draw out in the open air!
- Here you will find guidelines on how to approach landscapes, rivers and lakes, seascapes, trees and close-ups of leaves, flowers and more.

Note: Almost all the preparatory outline drawings done here are tidied-up roughs, and are done in HB pencil. The finished drawings use softer pencils for shading.

HILLS AND MOUNTAINS

COUNTRY LANDSCAPE

Step 1

Draw the outline of the hills first. Try to make them overlap as shown here. Don't worry if you have to rub out some lines and start again.

See how the hills are uneven? This makes them look more realistic.

A slightly curving path leads from the foreground towards the distant hills.

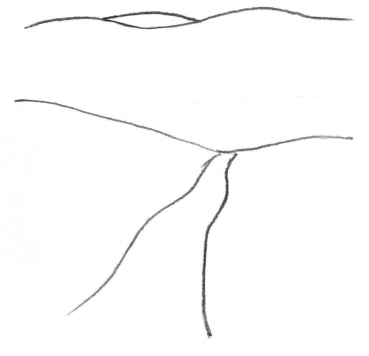

Step 2

Begin developing the scene by adding outlines:
- a fence that gets smaller as it goes into the distance.
- trees on the nearby hill.
- rocks and stones following the contours of the land.
- shrubbery in the foreground.
- a broken grassy ridge in the middle of the path.

Step 3

Add final detail and shading.

Draw in grass roughly. See on the left side of the path how the grass and fence wires follow the contours of the ground beneath.

Note: Get out into nature and see how the atmosphere affects the scenery near to you and far away.

Aerial Perspective
See page 56

ALPINE LANDSCAPE

Step 1

Draw an outline of the mountain, adding jagged edges to define its craggy sides.

Add the same type of mountains receding into the backround. Remember that the further objects are from us the lighter they are in tone.

Introduce shading to different areas, and draw in rough tree shapes.

Step 2

Give the foreground darker shading, to create depth.

Because the edges of the mountain are well defined, it follows that their shadows are as well. You can draw them as solid blocks of grey or black, depending how far they are from the sun.

Shade in the trees, darker and denser in the foreground. The tiny trees in the background are drawn just as elongated triangles.

Smooth out the shading by blending with your finger.

TREES

Trees come in lots of different shapes and sizes. The two main types are evergreen (for example, yew, pine, fir, holly), and deciduous (for example, oak, elm, birch, sycamore).

■ Evergreen Trees

NORWAY SPRUCE

Step 1

Draw the trunk from the ground up and make it narrow to a point at the top. Next, lightly draw the curving branches, not forgetting those branches facing towards you – this helps to make the tree look more like a three-dimensional object.

Step 2

Develop more curvy leaf shapes under the branches.

Step 3

Now add shading and further definition. The light source is overhead so the underside of branches should be darker. Remember to add a shadow on the ground.

Note: Follow the natural curves of the leaves when applying shading.

TWO YEWS

This magnificent tree is often found in graveyards.

Step 1

Common Yew   Irish Yew

- First draw rough circles to get the overall shapes of the trees.
- The common yew has long branches facing upwards. To develop this shape draw long ovals as seen at right.
- The Irish yew has branches that are almost horizontal. Draw slightly curving horizontal lines as shown.

Step 2

- Deciding where the light source is coming from, build up your shading and rub out any unnecessary rough lines.
  Add a couple of gravestones at this stage, as shown here.

Step 3

- Apply more shading and then tidy up, adding other gravestones, grass, and the wall of the graveyard.
- See how the angles of the gravestones are alternated? This is to give a balanced effect. If they were all facing the same way the composition of the picture would not be as good.

Hot Tip

When drawing trees and other foliage, take note of the construction of the leaves and branches. This gives you an idea of how to approach roughs that will make drawing the entire object a lot easier. For example, see how the deciduous tree on the opposite page and the two yew trees above are developed in completely different ways.

Deciduous Trees

WINTER

Step 1

Draw the trunk from the ground up, and split it into various branches as shown. Add smaller branches off the main ones.

Step 2

Lightly draw loose circles around the tree.

Step 3

Lightly shade in the circles and add twigs.

Roughen the circle edges with an eraser to make the tree look more natural.

Shade in the tree trunk.

SUMMER

Step 1 & 2

Repeat Steps 1 and 2 as described above.

Step 3

These circles are going to be the leafy areas of the tree, so fill them in with stronger shading.

Because the sun is overhead, apply more shading to the underneath of the circles.

Step 4

Add in the rough shapes of leaves over the circled outlines.

Blend the shading on the tree and shade in parts of the trunk as shown.

CLOUDS

As ever-changing elements of the sky, clouds greatly enhance and often complete a picture. Here are two series of clouds showing the effects of different materials.

PUFFY CLOUDS

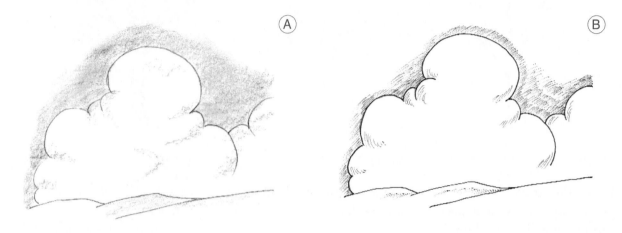

A. Using pencils

The outline of this puffy cumulus cloud was drawn first, and then a softer pencil applied for the faint rounded shapes within the cloud and for blended shading in the sky.

B. Using technical pens

A 0.35 pen was used for the outline and a 0.18 pen for the sky, which was done in single hatching.

RAIN CLOUDS

A. Using pencils

Darker clouds against clear sky were done in single hatching which was then blended. Darker shading is added to give the clouds substance.

B. Using technical pens

A 0.35 pen was used for outlines and a 0.18 pen for horizontal dark and light shading. To get the darker shading simply shade over the lighter shading with the same strength again.

SCATTERED CLOUDS

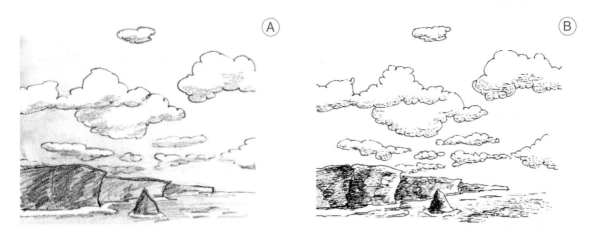

A. Using pencils

These cumulus clouds recede into the distance above cliffs. See how the undersides of the clouds are lightly blended. Make sure the cliffs are lighter in tone the further away they are.

B. Using technical pens

The outline is done with 0.35 pen and most of the shading was done in 0.18 with cross-hatching on the cliffs.

DISTANT CLOUDS

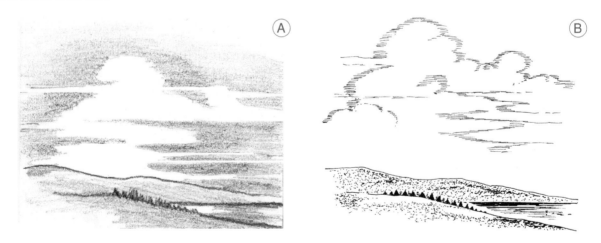

A. Using pencils

There are no outlines on these light clouds. Blend your shading carefully and give the background nearest the sky a different tone from the sky.

B. Using technical pens

Just thin strokes of a 0.25 pen are enough to give the impression of light clouds.

LAKES

Landlocked bodies of water, lakes are found in marshy land, on plains and in mountains and can be surrounded by foliage, or just rocks and grasses.

LAKE IN SPRINGTIME

Step 1

This outline drawing shows a head-on view of this wide lake. (If you wish it could also be a very wide river!) There is also an outline of rugged hills in the distance and some grasses and rocks in the foreground.

Step 2

The drawing is slowly developed, adding detail to the background and foreground. Closest to us, spring flowers with long leaves are also added.

Step 3

Shading and final detail are applied, along with light clouds in the distance.

MYSTERIOUS LAKE

Step 1

- This shows the outline of a section of a lake. In this view we are looking up along the lake shore to far-off mountains, which creates an interesting composition.
- The landscape has a natural mix of both foliage and bare terrain.

Step 2

- More detail is added. Notice the rocks and tall flowers in the foreground, and the leaves and branches on the trees in the middle ground.
- See where dark shadow has been applied on the rock area near the water? This is because the light source is top left and very little light reaches this area.
- Different levels of shading are drawn throughout the landscape.

Step 3

- As you can see, a lot more shading has been added, and any unnecessary outlines rubbed out.
- The area in the foreground is much more defined than the background.
- Notice that the mountain furthest away does not have an outline and is given very light shading.

In this final drawing some shading can still be seen as strokes or hatching.

Remember: When you copy these drawings or practise with your own drawings, it is up to you to choose whether to add lots of blending or give a rougher appearance.

◼ *Lakes from Imagination*

Drawing from imagination is fun! Try it yourself – just be sure to give your lake a realistic shape!

Step 1

- Here is the outline of a very small lake, showing roughed out positions of trees and shrubs.

Step 2

- Alder trees are found near lakes, and so here they are placed at the lake edges in such a way that they make a balanced composition.
- Shading and detail is developed.
- To bring an extra element to the picture, a couple of ducks are also added in the centre of the lake.

RIVERS AND WATERFALLS

MOUNTAIN RIVER

Step 1

- Here is the outline of a fast-flowing river rushing down a mountainside.
- See how the curving river leads the eye back up to the trees and mountains.
- Remember to balance your picture by creating different levels and placing objects at certain angles from each other. For example, notice the tree near to us on the left and other trees further away on the left and right.

Step 2

- Shading is added, making the foreground trees and boulders darker.

Step 3

- The light is coming from the right, so the highlights on the rocks are on the right. Very dark rocks with white highlights give the effect of wetness.
- The water is almost all frothy white because it is moving so fast. A few watery speed lines have been added to the foreground. And splashes on the rocks!
- The mountains have been lightly shaded and their outlines rubbed away.

CASCADING WATERFALL

Step 1

- Here is the outline of a river that becomes two waterfalls gushing over rocks.
- Note how the smaller waterfall falls into a dark pool, while the larger one continues to flow as a river.
- A little shading has been added.

Step 2

- Notice the slanted water lines in the waterfall on the right which clearly shows the direction and fast flow of water.
- Shade the back of the two waterfalls strongly to make them look dark.
- Highlight some of the nearer rocks with a few splashes of white to give a wet look.

HIGH WATERFALL

- This is a more simplified waterfall, created using just a few lines and shaded using single hatching.
- As an exercise, copy it and add more depth and detail.

■ *Reflections*

EARLY MORNING

- An easy way to achieve reflections is to use roughly drawn horizontal lines that do not fully join together.
- Sometimes water currents or light break up reflections. An eraser can be used to create this impression (*See* area A).
- Bear in mind that a reflection is often not a true representation of the real object – it may have a wavy or condensed appearance.
- The more still the water, the clearer and more complete the reflections.

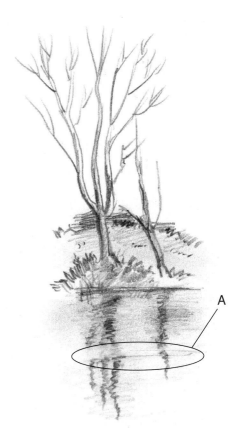

SEASCAPES

Here we look at sea cliffs and sandy shores, as well as waves.

■ *Coastal Sea*

TOWERING CLIFFS

Step 1

• Unfolding layers of sea cliffs receding far away are first roughly outlined. Remember your horizon line and convergence lines!

Perspective
See page 48

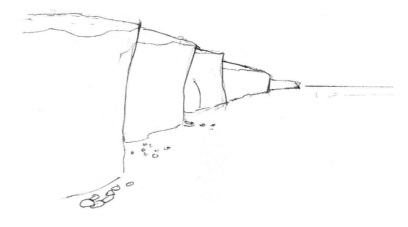

Step 2

• Now the shading begins. See how the frothy waves against the cliffs become narrower as they go into the distance.

Step 3

• The shading is built up further.
• To give the impression of waves further out at sea, dark jagged lines are drawn across the sea, and white horses added by using an eraser on parts of the sea to give the effect of movement.

Open Sea

A STORM BREWING

Step 1

- Above we have the outline of cross-currents at sea – the waves are rough and angry.
- The sky needs to be dramatic and indications of rays of light are added to what will be a gloomy backdrop.

Step 2

- Shading is developed throughout. The foreground waves are darker and have more definition than those in the distance.
- For the sky, clouds are blended and rays of light emphasised by using an eraser to create lines of pure white.

■ *Breaking Wave*

Waves can be difficult to draw, especially by observation as they move all the time! In saying this, it is excellent practice for your visual memory.

USING PENCILS

Step 1

This rough shows a crashing wave in a downward curve that bends back up as the wave turns into froth.

- Notice how the lines follow the wave's natural contours.

Step 2

- As the shading progresses, you can see that the inside of the wave is nearly translucent where the light shines through.
- Although the foam seems to be all white, there are actually areas of soft shading here and there to give it substance.
- The little waves in the foreground are drawn as overlapping curves.

USING TECHNICAL PENS

- This is the finished drawing of the same wave, but using technical pens.
- See how the froth is drawn as unfinished bubbles surrounded by an overall bubbly shape, except for the thin lines on the top of the wave and on the near side.

NATURE CLOSE-UPS

BLADDERWRACK SEAWEED

Bladderwrack seaweed can be seen on many seashores, only standing to attention when the tide is in. It is held to the rock by its root, called a holdfast (no kidding!).

Step 1

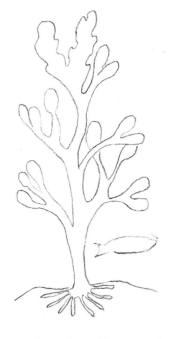

- This is our outline drawing. A fish is added so that straight away it is obvious that we are looking at an underwater scene.
- This is a good subject for practising your contour drawing. You can look at what you are drawing now and again (modified contour drawing) as you draw the shape.

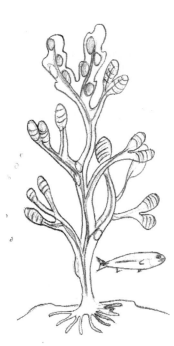

Step 2

- Further development of the drawing is done by adding in the bulbous leaves and bladders.
- The midribs of the branches are drawn and the shape of the fish is developed.
- A few air bubbles are sprinkled here and there.

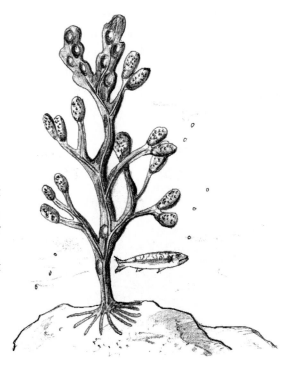

Step 3

- In the final drawing the seaweed is given a lot more shading. The light source is from the left, and shininess on the branches is conveyed by alternating light and dark shading.
- The friendly mackerel passing by gives a silent fin-wave!

HORSE CHESTNUT LEAF

This type of leaf is known as palmate because it has many leaflets.

Step 1

- Draw the outline very lightly as in the next step it will be amended.
- Try to keep a slightly curvy shape on every leaflet, and a pointy end to each one. Draw the centre rib line following the curve of each leaflet.

Centre rib

Step 2

- Draw strong little jagged lines all round the leaf. Take your time, ensuring the jagged edges face towards the tips of the leaflets.

Step 3

- The veins of the leaf are next. Count how many there are on a leaflet (in the middle leaflet there are ten) and draw evenly spaced markers along the entire centre rib.
- Then draw each vein line on either side of the centre rib out towards the edges of the leaflets.

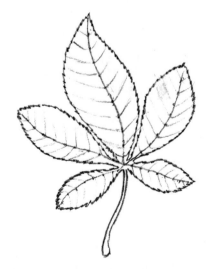

Step 4

- Different levels of shading give the finished leaf a realistic appearance.

CHERRY TREE IN SPRING

The cherry tree has beautiful small flowers every spring and cherries in autumn.

Step 1

- Here we have the rough outline of a cherry tree branch. See how the end of a branch is drawn? Each twig divides into a smaller twig over and over again.
- When you draw this branch yourself don't worry about it being totally accurate!

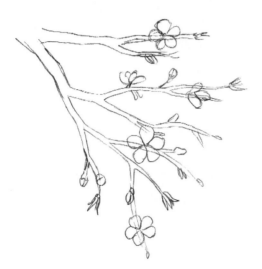

Step 2

- Now see how blossoms and buds are introduced on the tree. Each of the blossoms has five petals.

Step 3

- The final drawing. All the rough lines can now be rubbed out, or the rough redrawn on your lightbox.
- Blended shading is applied to the twig and flowers.
- Note the little ridge lines, which indicate where new growth begins on the twigs.

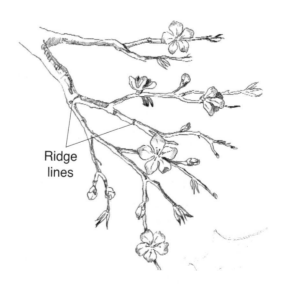

Ridge lines

ENDNOTE

A visit to the country, or a walk in a local park or garden can be a revelation when viewed with your new artistic awareness. And the same scene at various times of the day or in changing weather can produce different pictures.

Chapter 7
Cartoons

Overview

- Many people think there is only one way of drawing cartoons, and that you have to obey certain rules. Of course if you are working as a cartoonist for a cartoon or animation company they may need drawings to be done in a specific way. But apart from that, the way you draw cartoons is up to you!
- To see the limitless ways cartoons are used, just look around you. T-shirts, greeting cards, advertisements in magazines all display greatly different types of cartoons.
- Examples of various types of cartoons are on display in this chapter, some with step-by-step instructions. Practise drawing them and then do your own!

◼ *Audience*

- What audience are you aiming at? Teenagers and adults enjoy a diverse range of wacky, serious and complex cartoons while children prefer easy-to-understand funny characters.
- Whoever looks at your cartoon should be able to know straight away whether your characters are strong, sorrowful, cheerful, proud and so on. To do this, the emotions have to be far more theatrical than in real life – no need to be subtle!

◼ *Emotions*

- If you find it hard to draw a certain emotion, act it out in front of a mirror, or get someone to pose for you. Emotions in cartoons must be really over the top. See the two angry women below – the one on the left is too realistic; the one on the right – that's more like it!!

Anger

RAGE!

CARTOON PEOPLE

FACES

- Let's have a look at how faces can be developed from various head shapes and different eyes, noses, ears and mouths.
- Suggested roughs are given here, with their finished drawings below them. Remember that you can draw the roughs whichever way you want!

 *Guys Gallery*

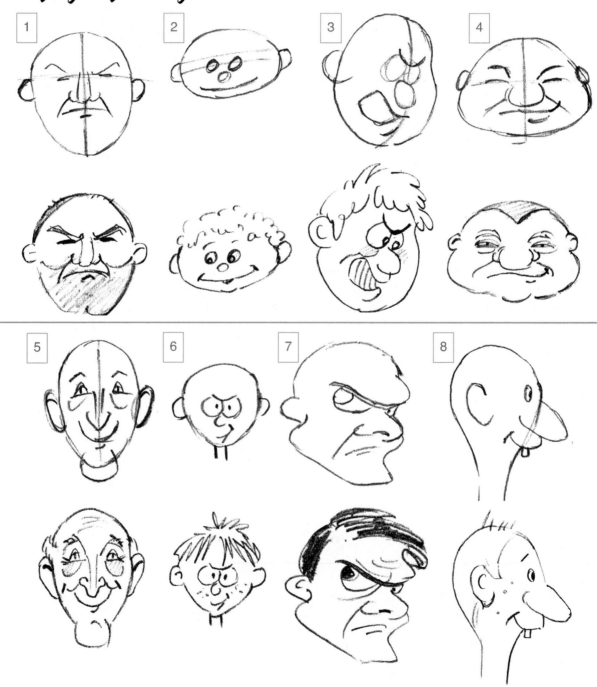

■ Gals Gallery

Hot Tip

You can use the guys rough head shapes and develop them into gal head shapes and vice versa.

BODIES

■ *Using Rounded Shapes and Scribbling*

Step 1

Using rounded shapes, draw a rough body and add the head, arms, hands, legs and feet.

Step 2

Develop, using scribbling, details such as facial features, clothes, background detail.

Step 3

Work up to the completed cartoon drawing, with extra detail and shading.

ROBINSON CRUSOE
See how in Step 2 his right arm is changed to hold a staff. Looks like Crusoe is a bit fed up on his tiny island!

Step 1   Step 2   Step 3

BOUNCER
Note the amendment of the arm shape in Step 2 and the surrounding landscape in Step 3.

Step 1   Step 2   Step 3

DIZZY BLONDE

This young woman has been given a classic hourglass figure and long blond hair.

Step 1   Step 2   Step 3

SHOPPING LADY

See how the shopper's clothes and bags develop and are altered in Step 2.

Step 1   Step 2   Step 3

MAN ON A MISSION

See how in Step 2 the scales are repositioned. They were too close to the man and the drawing would have looked too cramped if they were left in this position.

Step 1   Step 2   Step 3

CHOOSING CHARACTER TYPES

Depending on a storyline or the surrounding scene, a character's type can be re-used or interpreted in lots of different ways. Here are some examples:

Very happy . . . or listening to beautiful music . . . or just having eaten a delicious cake . . . or floating in a dream

Rock star wooing a large audience . . . or kid at a talent contest . . . or really bad singer who can't sing but giving it a go anyway!

Lazy person . . . or bored TV viewer . . . or at a party enjoying a quiet drink . . . or out of work and depressed

Shocked . . . or heartbroken . . . or very bad headache . . . or having made a terrible mistake

Suave businessman doing deal . . . or Mafia criminal boss . . . or rich man at elite social gathering

Exhausted student . . . or bored student at a lecture . . . or overworked man

SPECIAL EFFECTS

Effects are used all the time in cartoons and really bring characters alive!

Dashes can indicate embarrassment, surprise or even terror.

Water droplets can suggest a person is sweaty, overheated or anxious.

Speed lines indicate fast movement. Little puffs of smoke add to the effect.

Wavy lines are good at suggesting that a person is shivering. So is the shaded nose!

Speed lines can be combined with a burst bubble to indicate where the punch was given. Ouch! Remember, when drawing a punch like this, show the aftermath of the punch, and not the moment when the person actually makes contact with the victim.

Funny Walks

Try to keep your characters walking with their stride at its widest as seen in these drawings – it makes them look more cartoony.

Funny Runs

The same goes for the people in these drawings – you can stretch out their arms and legs as much as you like!

CHILDREN

- Remember to keep children's heads considerably larger than their bodies.
- For the 'cute' look, big eyes along with small hands and feet greatly helps.
- Don't forget children are not always sugar and spice – not always nice!

BABIES

- Tiny tots can be chubby and dimply, or cheeky and hard-edged.
- Have a look at the examples here and then create your own versions. **Note:** Your best reference is the real thing! So check out the children and babies in your neighbourhood and watch the way they act and are dressed.

Different arm positions are tried out in this rough.

CARTOON ANIMALS

*Cartoon animals can be drawn in as many ways as cartoon people.
Use the hints given for cartoon people in this section too.*

CREATING CHARACTERS

You can draw animals standing in a human-like way.

You can also draw animals in their normal poses but make
them look really funny by drawing them with human knees!

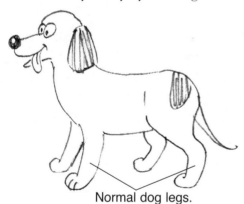

Normal dog legs.

Human knees!

Hot Tip

If you think you have run out of inspiration, doodle rough shapes as seen below. Any size and shape you like! Then fill them in. As well as making some wonderfully strange characters, this is a good exercise for stimulating your imagination and creativity.

HEADS

The animal heads below show you a variety of styles. Copy the heads you like best, building them up from roughs using any of the essential methods. Then create your own cartoon animal heads!

BODIES

Here are simple roughs to show the development of cartoon animal bodies. If you find it easier to do your roughs by scribbling or other methods, that's fine. Keep in mind it is by facial expressions that you can tell a lot about an animal.

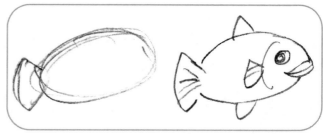

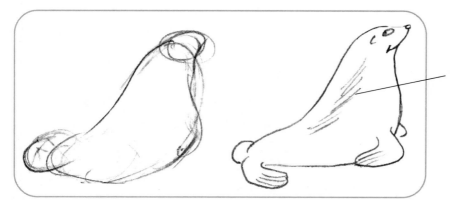

Single hatching on the skin gives the effect of shininess on this seal.

Sometimes a rough . . . is enough!

BABIES

- Like human babies, in general baby animals have larger heads. They can have either short legs (for example, dogs, cats, bears, lions, rabbits), or long legs (deer fawns, foals and all deer-like creatures).
- You can draw them with big or small eyes – look at the rabbit and squirrel and then look at the puppy and crazy little chick. See what works for you.

ANIMAL MAGIC

A selection of cartoon animals drawn in different styles are presented here. Now create your own!

ANTHROPOMORPHISM

*When we give an animal or object a human personality
or characteristics it is called anthropomorphism.*

- The 'mother' rabbit is drawn reasonably true to her rabbit body, whereas the 'bunny girl' next to her certainly isn't!
- The butterfly enjoying his dose of nectar is drawn with spindly arms and legs just like those on a real butterfly, except they are changed slightly so they look like human arms and legs.
- Have a go at drawing your own 'human' animals.

- Each drawing below is accompanied by a simple rough. Pick out one or two examples that you like from the gallery and then draw your own versions. Make them as crazy as you like!
- Select some mythical or fantasy creatures that are not included here, and draw them in your own style.

GALLERY

BARDOK THE BARBARIAN

If you find it difficult to draw a certain pose, copy that pose yourself in front of a mirror and use your visual memory to help you!

SELVA THE CENTAUR

Notice in the rough how the 'man' body and front legs form a nice 's' curve. This enhances the appeal of the final drawing.

TREE GOBLIN

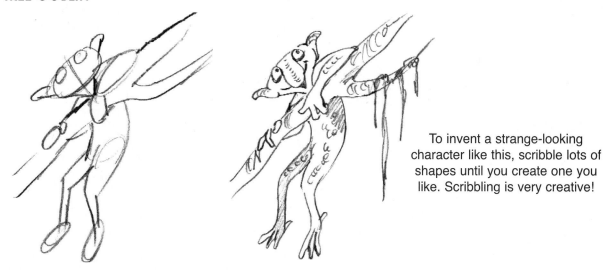

To invent a strange-looking character like this, scribble lots of shapes until you create one you like. Scribbling is very creative!

FIZZ THE WIZARD

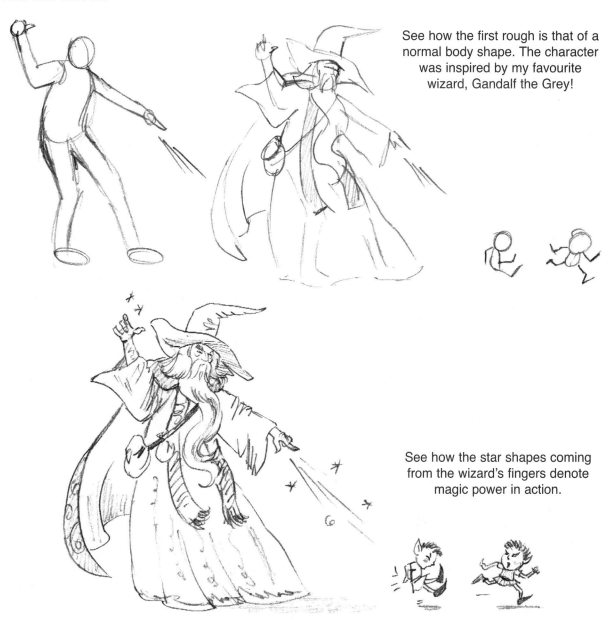

See how the first rough is that of a normal body shape. The character was inspired by my favourite wizard, Gandalf the Grey!

See how the star shapes coming from the wizard's fingers denote magic power in action.

FAERY

Again, the first rough is that of a simple body shape. As you add detail, remember to redraw as often as you need before reaching the finished drawing.

SNARGLE THE DRAGON

Can you see how the viewer is being 'told' that something has interrupted the dragon's reading?

Drawing from imagination usually means drawing a good deal of roughs, as you are working with little or no references!

ENDNOTE

The tips, demonstrations and advice in this chapter are to help you to develop your own original cartoons. Never feel you have to copy someone else's style to be good at cartoon drawing.

Chapter 8
Comic Strips

Overview

- Nowadays there are lots of comic books and strips available for children and adults. An art form in itself, the comic strip has had popular appeal for many years. Styles change over time, continually paving the way for new approaches that are at times wacky, provocative, satirical or just plain amusing!

- Here you will learn basic comic strip 'language', and see how the whole process is approached with many different examples. You'll also find out how to keep comic characters consistent by constructing model sheets, and various ways of thinking up stories.

- Remember that the following examples are done in my style and they are only meant to be guidelines: when you draw comic strips they are to be done in your own unique style!

■ *Frames*

- Each picture in a comic strip is called a frame. (It is also known as a panel.)
- The amount of detail you put in each frame depends on the type of comic strip.
- If you are in the middle of drawing a comic story and you change a location, give a fair amount of detail in that frame so the reader can understand what is going on. Frames that show new changes of scene are called **establishing shots**.
- The benefit of setting out frames properly, as in establishing a scene with the necessary detail, is that in the frames that follow, you can show minimal detail. This means that the reader can follow the story more quickly and easily.

■ *Text*

- Text in comic strips is usually shown in speech balloons, thought balloons and sound effects.
- Make sure you give enough space for text, but do not allow it to take over from the artwork.
- Keep the dialogue short and direct.
- Think ahead! Put the person who speaks first on the left of the frame, since people from the Western world read from left to right. If your frame is taller than wide, the speech bubbles to be read first should be at the top.

SAMPLE COMIC STRIP

On the opposite page is a comic strip of Charlie the Curious Cat and an explanatory breakdown of all the features. The final artwork of this strip was drawn using a felt-tip marker.

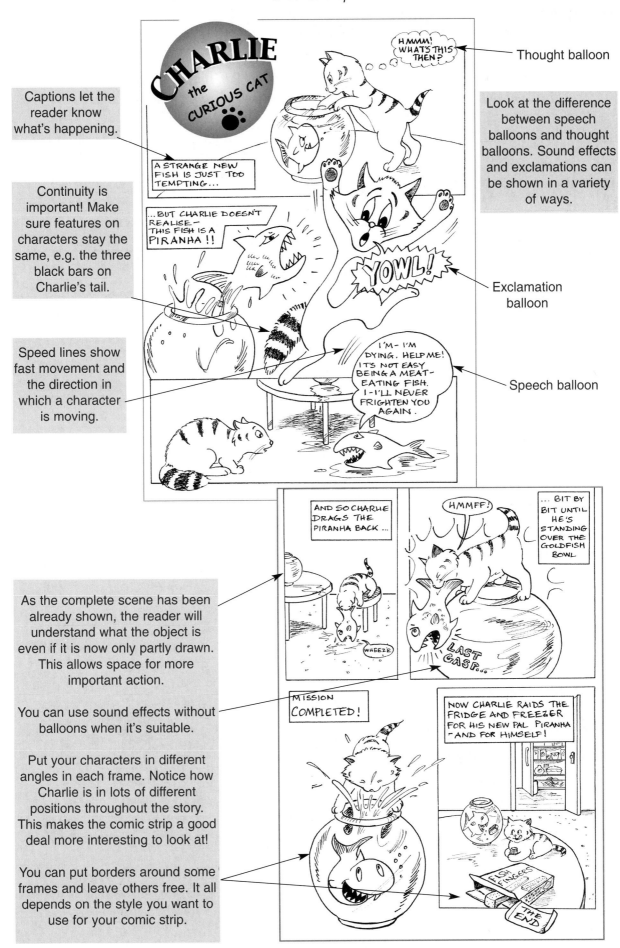

Captions let the reader know what's happening.

Continuity is important! Make sure features on characters stay the same, e.g. the three black bars on Charlie's tail.

Speed lines show fast movement and the direction in which a character is moving.

Thought balloon

Look at the difference between speech balloons and thought balloons. Sound effects and exclamations can be shown in a variety of ways.

Exclamation balloon

Speech balloon

As the complete scene has been already shown, the reader will understand what the object is even if it is now only partly drawn. This allows space for more important action.

You can use sound effects without balloons when it's suitable.

Put your characters in different angles in each frame. Notice how Charlie is in lots of different positions throughout the story. This makes the comic strip a good deal more interesting to look at!

You can put borders around some frames and leave others free. It all depends on the style you want to use for your comic strip.

TYPES OF COMIC STRIP

The examples on the following pages show different approaches to drawing comic strips. By looking through them you may see which type or types you would like to try out yourself.

■ *Young Children's Comic*

The sequence below could be an excerpt from a story. The setting is one a young child would be familiar with, and the storyline is easy to understand.

- The characters are animals with human characteristics, which children like. The narrative is under each frame in the final comic strip below.
- The frames are set out in a simple way, and each picture is at a different angle so that the story looks interesting.

SUNNYLAND TALES
A Day Off for Ben & Flopsy

Outline Drawing / Technical Pen

Finished Art + Black Paint

Flopsy Rabbit rushes up to the bus stop. Ben Beaver is already there. 'Just in time!' Flopsy gasps.

The school bus arrives just as Flopsy finishes speaking, but . . .

. . . instead of stopping to pick up Flopsy and Ben, it drives straight past them!

Older Children's Comics

In the comic strip below, we hear what the characters are thinking and saying by means of speech and thought balloons. Captions are also included. Note the different shapes of frames, and the jagged inset of our anti-hero.

RAYNARDO THE RASCALLY FOX
Raynardo gets his come-uppance!

Outline Drawing / Technical Pen

Finished Art + Black Paint

■ Teenage or Adult Graphic Novel

Realistic artwork is the basis for this type of comic strip. In this page from a potential story, you can see how the sizes and shapes of frames change and overlap. Interesting angles are used throughout – a close-up, a long shot from above etc.

RENEGADE
THE RETURN

First Rough

Finished Outline

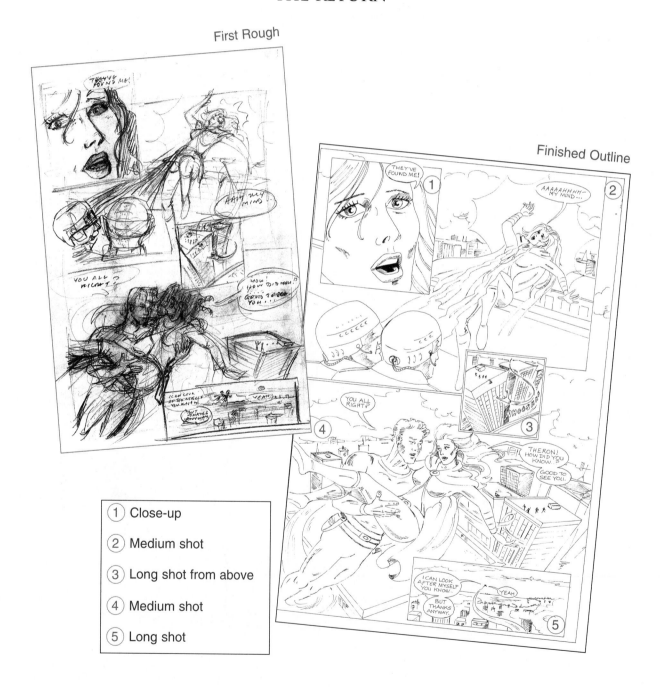

1. Close-up
2. Medium shot
3. Long shot from above
4. Medium shot
5. Long shot

Finished Art + Black Paint

◼ *Gag Strip*

*Simplicity is the key. There is no need to be too elaborate with the artwork,
as the intention is to get the message across clearly.*

HAROLD
THE HAPLESS HYPNOTIST

Outline Drawing / Technical Pen

Finished Art + Black Paint

MODEL SHEETS

If you are drawing a comic story of any considerable length, it is a good idea to draw your chosen characters on model sheets first. This way you can see what they look like from different angles, which is important for consistency.

GRAN'S GANG

Here is a sample model sheet of a great character, Hell's Gran!

Here is a separate model sheet with the other characters in the story, to show the comparison of different heights.

Hell's Gran   Dawg   Snip   Charlotte   Melvin

THINKING UP A STORY

1. LET YOURSELF DAYDREAM

Pick a topic – any topic! – and let your mind play with it, allowing your thoughts to weave a story.
Use trigger questions: What happened? Why? Where?
Here is how I thought up a story called *Night from Day*.

Pick a topic: I thought of . . . the sun.

Question: What could happen to the sun?

Answer: It falls out of the sky onto the earth and burns a hole all the way to Australia and out the other side.

Question: Now why would the sun do this?

Answer: Because it is fed up hanging around in the sky all the time.
I let my mind play with this for a while, and my imagination began to flow. The story continued . . . With tact, friendship and compromise, the sun strikes a deal with a sympathetic human. A big cloak is hung in the sky so the sun can get a rest once in a while. Balance and harmony is restored!

The sketches below are an interpretation of this story.

2. IN EVERYDAY LIFE, TAKE SPECIAL NOTE OF SOCIAL SITUATIONS AND CONVERSATIONS.

You will be surprised at the wealth of interesting and humorous information you can pick up. Here are a few pointers:

People chatting at bus stops/with assistants in shops; friends walking or talking in parks, pubs, coffee shops; seeing how people behave in their cars, on trains, in public places like post offices and banks; families and relatives interacting . . .

The list is endless!

3. TV, RADIO AND NEWSPAPERS CONTAIN TITBITS THAT CAN SET YOUR CREATIVITY AFIRE.

An example I call to mind is a sketch on a TV comedy show some time ago that could be transferred nicely into a comic strip. It went something like this:

Various people come by to peek into a pram, oohing and aahing. (You just see the profile of the pram.) Another person comes along and leans into the pram to admire the baby like all the others. Suddenly the person is dragged into the pram head first until he vanishes, gobbled up! The sketch ends with the pram emitting a very loud belch.

4. CREATE POINTS FOR YOUR STORY

This method is more organised and sets everything out step by step. In the example below I leave the ending open for you to finish.

1   A terrible accident happens at a chemical plant. Source is unknown.
2   Three experts (two men, one woman) attempt to find out what caused it, and in so doing discover a huge conspiracy.
3   One member of their team is a baddie and tries to sabotage the other two.
4   After a couple of narrow escapes, the goodies discover a secret cavern, which is the base of the misguided genius they are searching for.
5   Now . . . add your own ending!

ENDNOTE

- Keep handy references in an album or scrapbook. Be on the alert for potential photographs and pictures of objects you could use in your comic strips.
- It is also a good idea to collect different types of comic strips and graphic novels to study their techniques. But remember to keep your own individual style!

'I told you before, Einstein, no scribbling on the blackboard!'

Chapter 9
Animation
Drawings that Move!

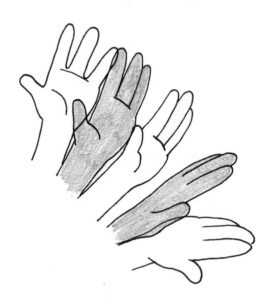

Overview

- Animation was recognised as an art form at the beginning of the twentieth century, and was made popular by Walt Disney. Over the years, basic techniques have been developed and refined, which are to this day used by animators throughout the world.
- The following pages guide you through some of these basic techniques, which include creating a flip book, making movements look realistic and funny, and showing how humans and animals run or walk on the spot. You will also learn how to make a lightbox.
- This fascinating art involves a good deal of patience, so take your time and have fun.

HOW TO GET STARTED

A lot of animation is done on computers these days, but to get a grasp of the basics it is good to practise your drawings with pencil and paper.

■ *Animation Desk*

The picture below shows a standard animation desk with built-in animation peg bars. The paper is punched so that it fits neatly over the peg bars.

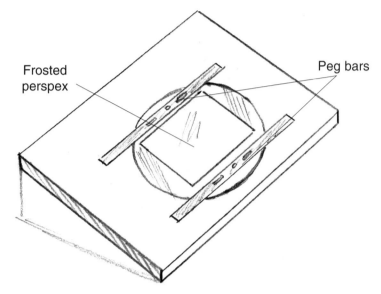

Frosted perspex

Peg bars

■ *Working with a Lightbox*

• All of the animation exercises in this book were done on separate sheets of paper using a lightbox. With peg bars and punched animation paper I was able to flick the pages back and forth to ensure the movements were OK.

• You can buy individual peg bars and punched animation paper in some good art suppliers. If you cannot access these materials locally, just put sheets of paper on the lightbox taped at the lower edges so you can flick the paper back and forth. Use invisible tape or sticky post-it sheets.

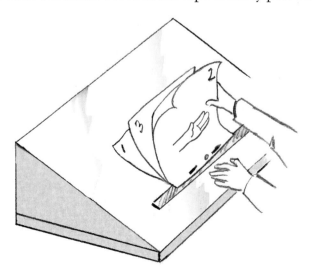

CREATE YOUR OWN LIGHTBOX

- Lightboxes are very handy – not just for animation, but for tidying up all kinds of drawings and roughs. Good graphic art suppliers stock lightboxes of different sizes. They can be expensive, so shop around.
- The other more economical option is to make one – or get someone to make it for you! Anyone who has a basic knowledge of woodwork will find the instructions below easy to follow.

MATERIALS REQUIRED

- 6mm plywood or veneered chipwood
- Wood beading 6mm (1/4 inch)
- Frosted or clear perspex
- Screws and wood glue
- Strip light

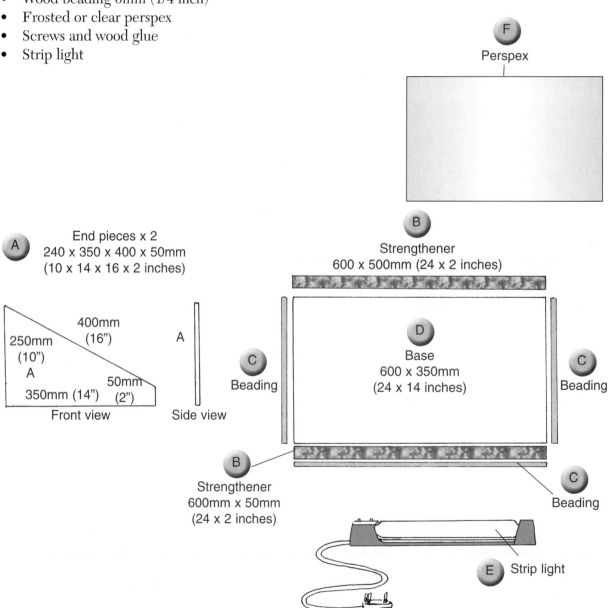

F Perspex

A End pieces x 2
240 x 350 x 400 x 50mm
(10 x 14 x 16 x 2 inches)

400mm (16")
250mm (10")
A
350mm (14") 50mm (2")
Front view

A
Side view

B Strengthener
600 x 500mm (24 x 2 inches)

C Beading

D Base
600 x 350mm
(24 x 14 inches)

C Beading

C Beading

B Strengthener
600mm x 50mm
(24 x 2 inches)

E Strip light

■ *Instructions*

- Cut the plywood to the sizes given.
- Screw and glue the end pieces to the base.
- Add strengtheners to the top and front of the box.

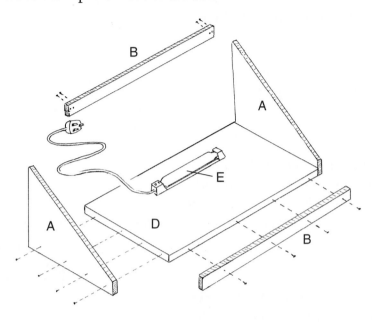

- Nail the beading around three sides of the box, leaving the top edge free.
- Cut the perspex to size and slide it into the beaded frame.
- Attach the strip light near the **rear** of base with screws. The position is important – light will be displaced better and your working area will not get too hot.

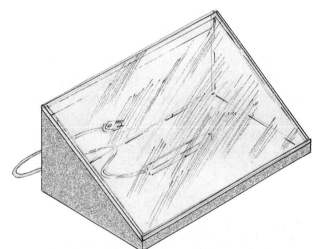

- Your new lightbox is ready for use!

MAKING A FLIP BOOK

After you have carried out some of the exercises in this chapter it's a worthwhile exercise to make flip books. It will help you see how animation works and to see that your drawings really do move!

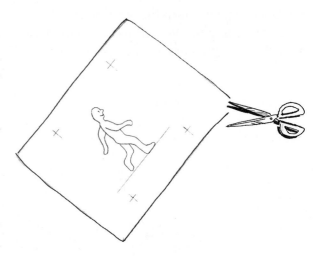

- Copy the sequences onto the thickest paper that will go through a photocopier.

- Then cut out the drawings and use the registration marks to perfectly line up each drawing. Make sure you leave extra space at the left edge of the drawing sequences.

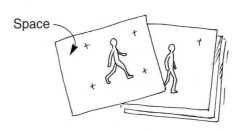

Space

- With a strong stapler, staple the drawings together at the left edge. Then simply flip the pages back and forth and see animation in motion!

A couple of sequences in this chapter do not have registration marks (figure kicking, flag flapping). If you want to make them into flip books, use the stationary elements within the sequences as registration markers, for example, the still foot, and the flagpole.

Hot Tip

- Access a VCR and play a cartoon on it. Replay sections of it frame by frame. You will be amazed as you see the clever techniques animators use to achieve funny and believable movements for their characters.
- Sometimes it is hard to imagine how a movement works until you do it yourself, so get a full-length mirror and act it out. Or get a friend or relative to act it out for you! It is also a good idea to have a small mirror nearby for checking your own face and hand movements.
- When you begin to draw your own animation sequences, scribble out everything roughly first. Give yourself lots of time to get your movements right and only then tidy up your drawings.

KEY DRAWINGS AND INBETWEENS

THE TURNING HAND

Step 1

Tape a sheet of paper onto your lightbox. (Make sure to tape just the bottom part!) You can also use a peg bar to hold your paper (see picture at bottom of page).

Next, put registration marks (little crosses) at each corner. And see the small grid at the bottom of the paper? This tells us that there are three drawings in this sequence. The first and last drawings are called **key drawings**, as they are the main drawings. Drawing number two is called an inbetween. Now draw your first key drawing, a hand. Let's call it **H1**.

Step 2

Put another sheet of paper over the first one. You should be able to see H1 clearly. First, copy the registration marks from H1. Now draw the last key drawing. Call it **H3**.

Step 3

Put a third sheet over the other two. You should be able to see the two other drawings underneath.

Again, copy the registration marks. Then, measuring as best you can, draw a hand that is halfway between the other two drawings. Take special note of how the 'inbetween' hand position will look compared with the other two. Call this hand **H2**.

The picture on the right shows H2, the finished inbetween, on top of H1 and H3.

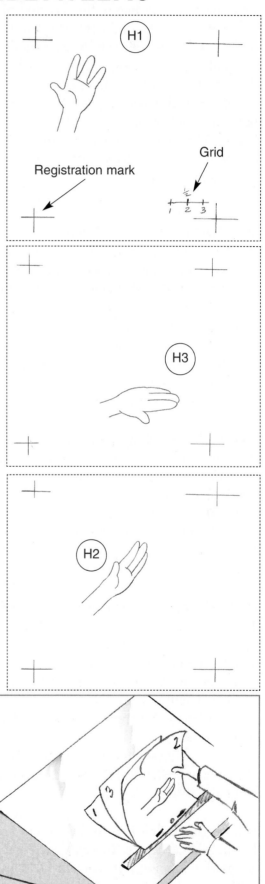

Registration mark

Grid

163

Step 4

Rearrange the drawings so they are now placed back on your lightbox in the order H1, H2, H3. Line up all the registration marks on each sheet of paper.

Hold the sheets loosely in one hand and slowly flip them back and forth. As the three images flash in front of your eyes, the hand appears to turn from upright to flat – and back up again!

Note: The three hands on this page are placed together on one sheet just so you can see the movements clearly.

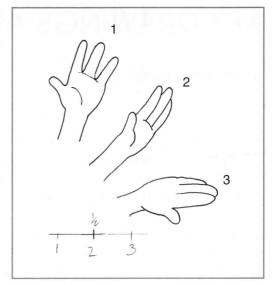

SLOWING DOWN THE ACTION

By adding more inbetweens at the start and end of the sequence, the hand movement appears to move more slowly. (See the shaded hands, H2 and H4.)

See the grid. The halfway point inbetween we knew before as H2 is now renamed H3, because we want to put an extra drawing, or inbetween, on either side of it.

When you are finished the new inbetweens, rearrange the drawings in the order H1 to H5 and flip to see the movement!

Note: When creating an inbetween, you just need two drawings underneath to work from: for example, H1 and H3 to get H2. When finished with these, use H3 and H5 to get H4.

Don't worry if you can't draw your inbetweens correctly at first – be patient and go over them as many times as you need to get them right.

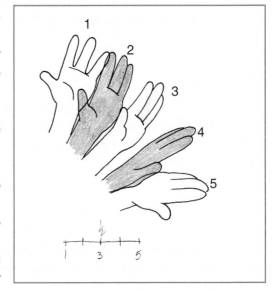

MAKING THE ACTION LOOK MORE REAL

To do this, we start the movement slowly and end it slowly. This means we need to add an extra inbetween at either end of the sequence.

Check out the revised grid on this sequence. Our previous halfway point, H3, is now H4, and the other drawings from the previous sequence have also been renumbered.

A new inbetween is drawn between H3 and H1, and also between H5 and H7. (See the shaded hands, H2 and H6.)

Rearrange the drawings in the correct order of H1 to H7 and flip as before. You may need some practice to get used to flipping, but keep at it! It is great to see the final images in motion!

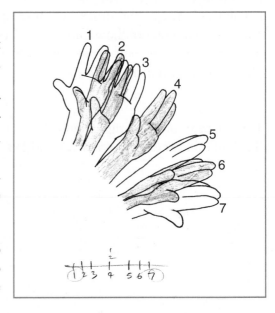

SQUASH AND STRETCH

Just about everything in this world is affected by gravity. In animation it pays to use the squash and stretch technique as it really helps to give a realistic look to characters.

THE BOUNCING BALL

Sequence 1

- This sequence shows how a bouncing ball looks when moving at the same speed all the time. When finally viewed in a flip book it would look very unrealistic.

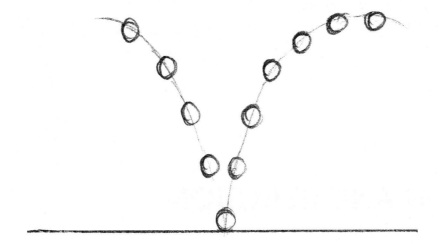

Sequence 2

- This sequence shows the bouncing ball moving fast and slow. See how the ball changes shape as it dives downwards to the ground, and then back up again? Yes, it may look a bit exaggerated and overdone but this sequence will look much more realistic in a flip book than the sequence above.

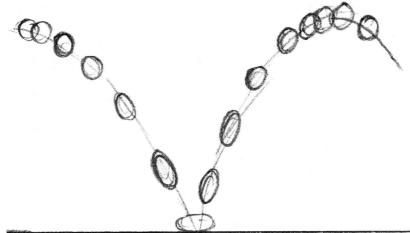

ARCS

When humans and animals move, a lot of the time it is in curves and arcs and not in straight lines.

THE MOVING ARM

See how the woman's arm points. Notice also the different distances between drawings!

- Look back to the first exercise, **The Turning Hand**, and see how arcs are used even in this simple movement.

ACTION AND REACTION

THE KICK

- As well as **arcs** displayed in this sequence, here you also see **action and reaction** or **anticipation**. This involves a movement *before* the main movement, in this case the leg being swung backwards before being then swung forward in the kick.

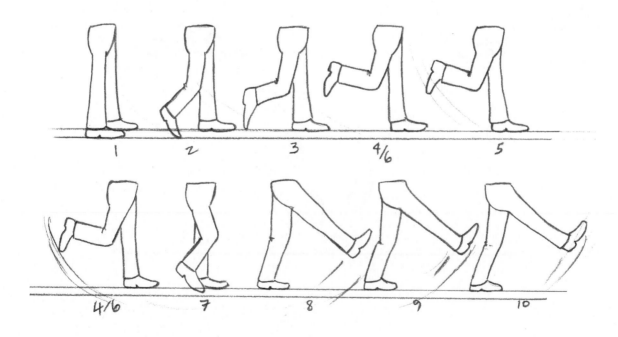

THE TAKE

- It can be quite funny to watch cartoon people or animals being surprised. Look at this sequence of Terry Terrapin. Notice how **squash and stretch** is used along with **action and reaction** to create the atmosphere. The most extreme pose where Terry is most stretched with fright, is the actual '**take**'.

TERRY TERRAPIN

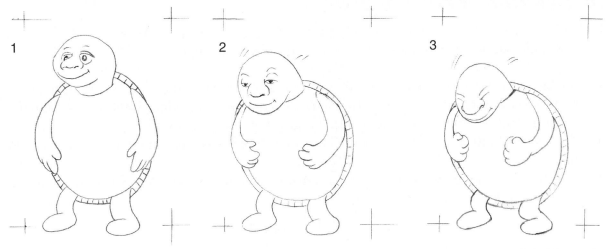

Terry is in normal pose in Picture 1, and then fully squashed down into anticipation crouch in Picture 3.

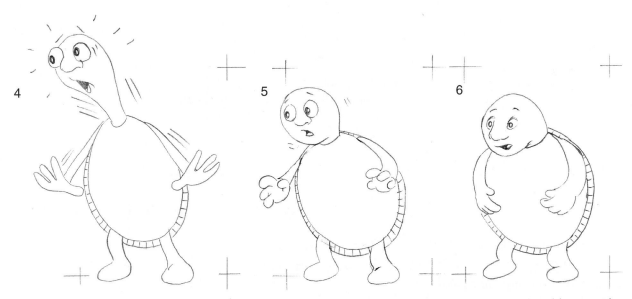

In Picture 4 Terry stretches into his take.

In Picture 5 and Picture 6 Terry springs back into his normal shape. After Picture 6 he returns to Picture 1.

CYCLES

A cycle is a repeated action of a person, animal or object. As you can imagine, cycles are used all the time in animation, and are adapted in many different ways. For example, cycles can comprise a complete stride or run (for a person), or a complete wingbeat (for a bird).

■ *Human Walk Cycle*

Let's go through a 12-drawing human walk cycle, featuring Mister Anony Muss. (See the cycle on the opposite page.) There are two steps in a complete stride.

- Do the extreme drawings first. These are the drawings where the front foot has just been placed on the ground at the start of a step. In this sequence they are drawings 1 and 7. Also note that when the foot swings forward, the opposite arm swings forward as well.
- Then do the **halfway point** drawings. These are where the person is in mid-step. In this case they are drawings 4 and 10.
- The other drawings that complete the cycle are not exact **inbetweens** so you have to be careful! The grid for drawing the full cycle is as follows:

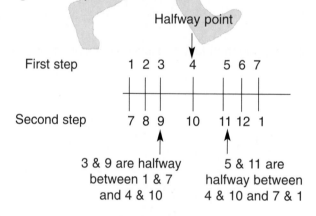

If you are writing the drawings in continuous sequence it looks like this:

1   2   3   4   5   6   7   8   9   10   11   12   and back to 1 again.

- It is also useful to note that 1 and 7, 2 and 8, 3 and 9, 4 and 10 as well as 5 and 11 are the same position but with opposite hands and feet!
- You will also see that with each mid-step (Drawings 4 and 10) the head gently bobs up. Then his head bobs down as the foot is planted on the ground (Drawings 1 and 7).
- If you make a flip book of this cycle you will see the character walking on the spot!

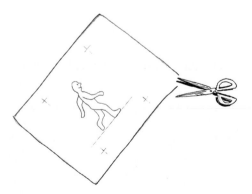

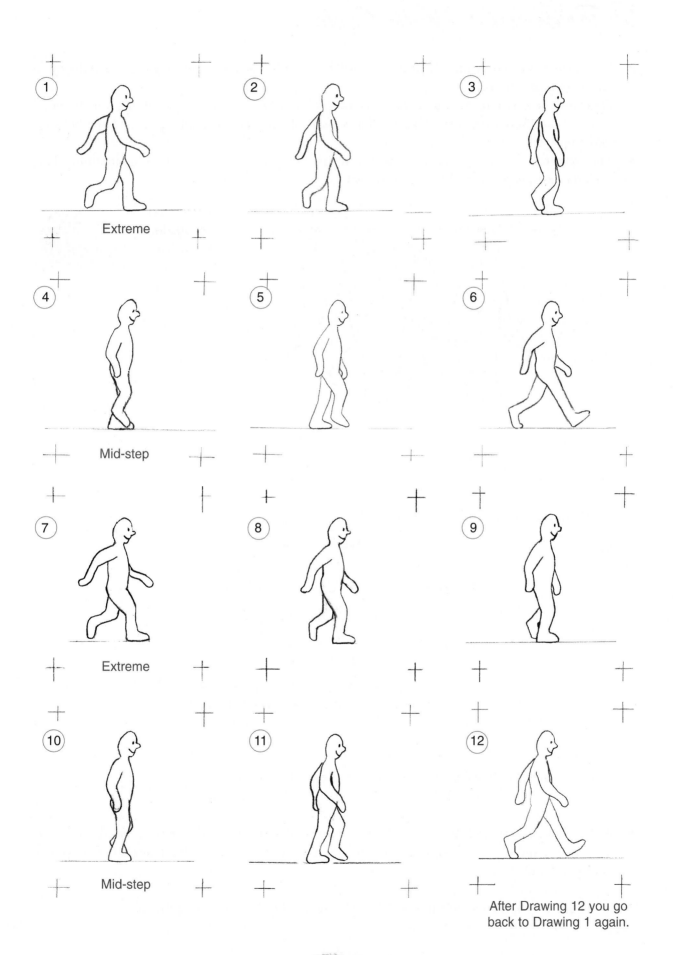

After Drawing 12 you go
back to Drawing 1 again.

Perspective Walk Cycle

- Decide how many drawings the full stride will be. In this case it is eight drawings. (See the cycle on the opposite page.)
- Determine the size of Mister A. Nother and the path he is going to take. Lines for the head and feet positions are drawn. These will stay basically the same except when his head bobs up mid-step.
- The **extreme** drawings (1 and 5) are drawn first. They are drawn along a receding line. This fixes the perspective for all the other drawings.

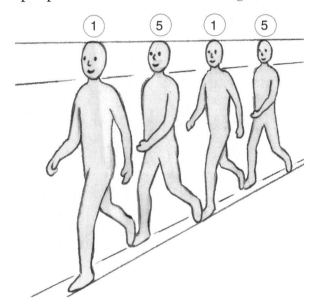

Perspective
See page 48

The grid for drawing the full cycle is as follows:

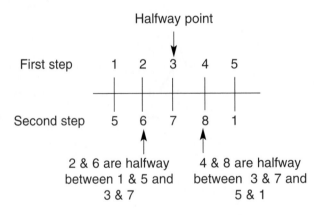

If you are writing the drawings in continuous sequence it looks like this:
1   2   3   4   5   6   7   8 and back to 1.

- Notice how Drawings 1 and 5 are the same finished step, but with opposite hands and feet. Drawings 2 and 6, 3 and 7 as well as 4 and 8 are pairs of the same position, again with opposite hands and feet.

Note: The nearer someone gets to you, the faster he or she will seem to approach!

■ *Perspective Walk Cycle*

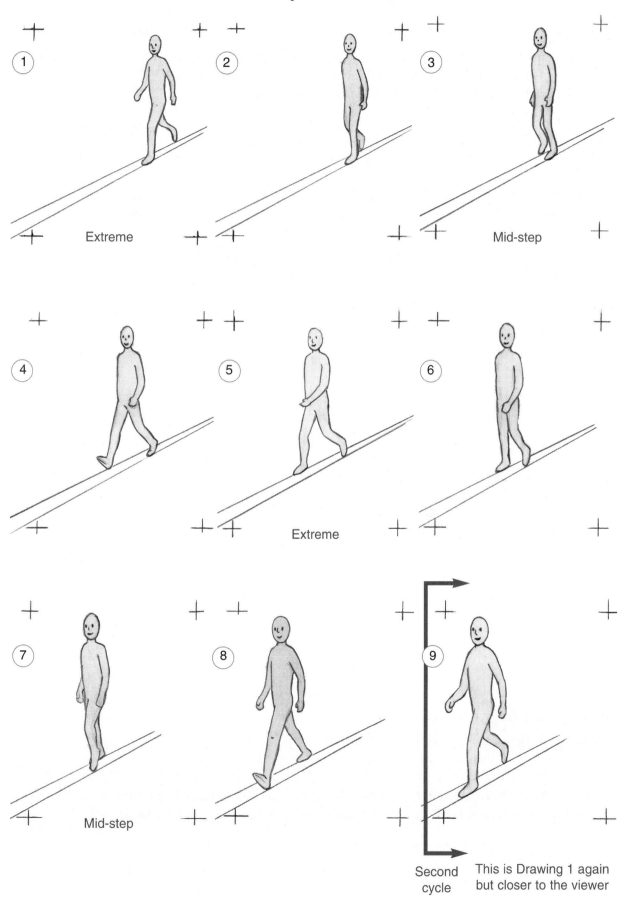

1. Extreme
2.
3. Mid-step
4.
5. Extreme
6.
7. Mid-step
8.
9. Second cycle

This is Drawing 1 again but closer to the viewer

Cartoon Run Cycle

ELFIE THE ELF

Here is an eight-cycle run of Elfie the Elf. See how each full step takes four drawings, and that Elfie's two feet come off the ground in Drawing 3 and its opposite, Drawing 7. Notice that only the arms change to indicate stepping out with the opposite foot.

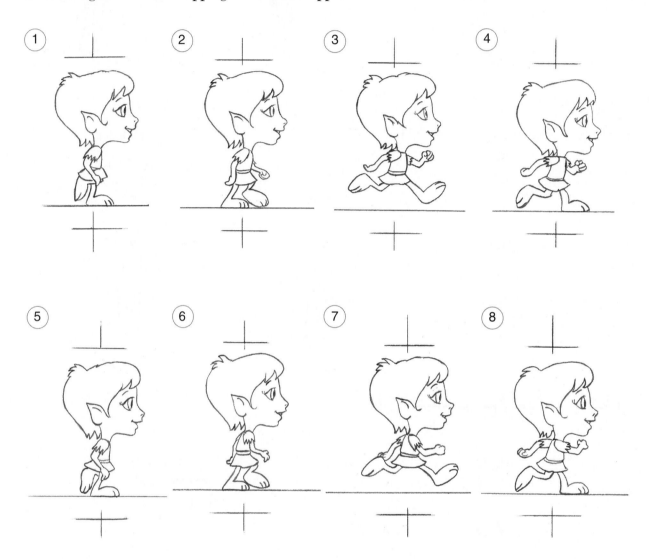

Hot Tip

Are you ready to do cycles for your own characters? Just keep the same basic movements that you see in the examples here and then adjust the height, alter the face and body features and don the character with whatever clothes you want!

Animal Run Cycle

Here is a cat in profile running after an elusive mouse! This time the cycle is seven drawings.

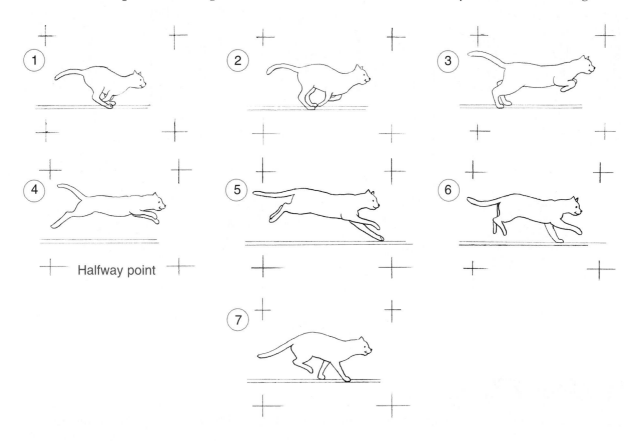

Halfway point

THE WAVE EFFECT

*This technique is often used as a cycle, and occurs in various movements.
When seen onscreen wave movements are smooth and flowing.*

Dogtail Wagging

Copy each tailwag onto a separate sheet of paper, keeping the registration marks. Then make your own flip book – watch that tail go!

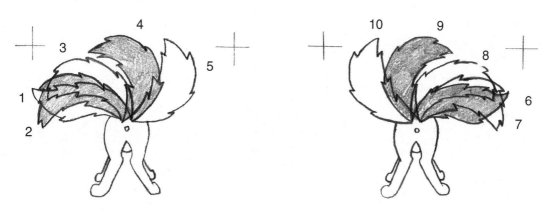

■ *Flag Waving*

Draw each flag position carefully in this nine-step cycle.

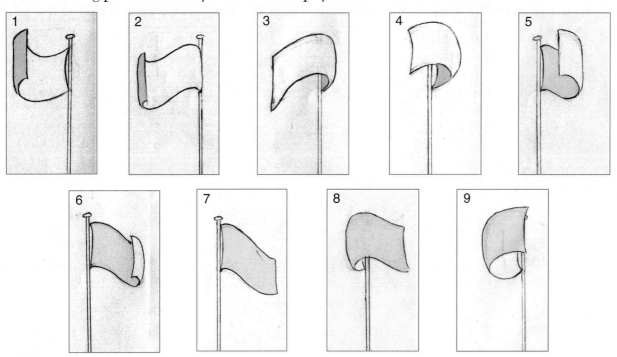

■ *Bird Flying*

When you complete this cycle of the bird flying, repeat it several times to keep him in the air!

GLOSSARY

align – to line up one object evenly with another

angle – (i) the shape formed by two straight lines that meet; (ii) what something looks like from a certain point of view

caption – short text or comment accompanying a picture that explains its content

characteristic – way of acting or behaving according to personality

consistency – keeping a feature or features on a person or object the same throughout a story

contour – the form or outline of an object

depth – the distance downwards, backwards or inwards

diagonal – slanted line upwards or downwards from right to left or left to right

dialogue – characters in conversation

enhance – to make something look better

feature – item in a picture

finished artwork – the final stage of a drawing, either as tidied-up outline or filled in with shading etc.

focus – area in a picture you want a viewer to give most attention

form – structure of a picture, drawing or work of art, as distinguished from its content

freehand – not using a ruler

harmony – a drawing or picture that has elements within it that are pleasing to the eye

horizontal line – a line straight across

impression – a picture that is based on a subjective observation rather than an accurate form or structure

indicator line – a line that helps the artist to get correct measurements in a drawing

light source – the direction from which light falls on objects

marker – short guidelines or dots that help measure an object. *See* indicator line

measuring gauge – indicator line with markers on it

mid-tone – not too dark, not too light

narrative – text that explains various pictures or frames

original picture – (i) the actual picture drawn or painted by an artist, not a copy or reproduction; (ii) a picture referred to at the beginning of a text or exercise

outline – a drawing with no shading or paint added to fill in the object

overlap – an object that partly covers another

posture – the way a person holds him, or herself, whether standing, sitting or lying down

preparatory drawing – drawing before doing a second picture, which has more details or is more complete

prop(s) – object(s) surrounding a model in life drawing

proportions – dimensions and size of objects

registration marks – little crosses placed around animation drawings, enabling the animator to line up one drawing over another with precision.

repose – face relaxed and not moving

rough – the first attempt at creating a drawing

sequence – a series of drawings that show a complete pattern or action

setting – the location where a scene or a story is placed

structure – the basic make-up of an object

temporary line – lightly-drawn pencil guideline that is erased at the final artwork stage

tone – quality of shade or tint

vertical line – a line straight down

BIBLIOGRAPHY

Anatomy for Artists – The Leonardo Collection. Published by Vinciana

Edwards, Betty. *Drawing on the Right Side of the Brain.* HarperCollins, 1993

Muybridge, Eadweard. *Animals in Motion.* Dover Publications, 1957

Murray, Peter and Linda. *The Penguin Dictionary of Art & Artists.* Penguin Books, 1983

Thomas, Frank; Johnston, Ollie. *The Illusion of Life – Disney Animation.* Abbeville Press, 1981

INDEX